# THE LAND OF
# FLYING LAMAS

An engineer from the University of California, Berkeley, and a trekker by choice, Gaurav Punj has been exploring the Indian Himalaya since 2006. Through his books and his venture, Connect with Himalaya, he aims to do his bit to spotlight the lesser known Himalaya and demystify trekking as an activity everyone can enjoy.

# THE LAND OF FLYING LAMAS

**& OTHER REAL TRAVEL STORIES FROM THE INDIAN HIMALAYA**

# GAURAV PUNJ

First published by Tranquebar, an imprint of westland ltd, in 2013

Published by Tranquebar, an imprint of Westland Books, a division of Nasadiya Technologies Private Limited, in 2024

No. 269/2B, First Floor, 'Irai Arul', Vimalraj Street, Nethaji Nagar, Alapakkam Main Road, Maduravoyal, Chennai 600095

Westland, the Westland logo, Tranquebar and the Tranquebar logo are the trademarks of Nasadiya Technologies Private Limited, or its affiliates.

Text copyright © Gaurav Punj, 2013

'Trekking: The Way of the Wise,' copyright © Rujuta Diwekar, 2013

Illustrations copyright © Shreyas Navare, 2013

ISBN: 9789360453251

10 9 8 7 6 5 4 3 2 1

The views and opinions expressed in this work are the author's own and the facts are as reported by him, and the publisher is in no way liable for the same.

All rights reserved

Typeset by Ram Das Lal, New Delhi

Printed at Saurabh Printers Pvt. Ltd

No part of this book may be reproduced, or stored in a retrieval system, or transmitted in any form or by any means, electronic, mechanical, photocopying, recording, or otherwise, without express written permission of the publisher.

## Foreword

Any trip to the mountains, to the Himalaya or otherwise, generates a variety of experiences, from the mundane to the unforgettable, and interactions within the group and with locals on the way create memories worth holding on to and narrating at the next campfire. You follow directions, look at the peaks and enjoy beauty, but it's the human interactions, which we call stories, that let you understand the land and its people most intimately.

This is what Gaurav Punj, the author, has done in this book, and he is eminently qualified to write such a book. An engineer by education, corporate honcho in his first avatar, he decided to give up the humdrum, but well-paying life, for the uncertainties of mountains as a means of living. In a way it was in his blood, having been born in the foothills of the Himalaya, in the Shivalik range. Perhaps to him the high profile CV appeared miniscule compared to the grandeur of the mountains. But while roaming the hills your banker cannot help, so he set up his own company, appropriately named 'Connect with Himalaya'. Since then he has not looked back, being connected with the mountains all through the year. He enjoys it, as I have seen him in action once in the mountains.

For lifelong passion for mountains there are a few hurdles. You finish education and you are supposed to toe the line; join work or business. If you still continue to trek, then various circumstances are likely to challenge your chosen life. For the survivors, the hardest hurdle to cross is choosing a partner with whom to live the rest of your life. A companion with less understanding of your passion can lead to many conflicts between the social life in a city vs. the hard life of mountains. Gaurav has succeeded in solving this riddle by choosing Rujuta, a celebrated author and a passionate trekker herself, as his life partner. Their marriage, realized in a small temple in a remote Himalayan village, is an example of their love for the Himalaya.

This book contains many things of interest to a Himalayan lover and trekker. There are maps and trivia, suggestions of local service providers for those interested in travelling to the places covered in the book and, what I like most, references to read and research further for a discerning trekker. Many important aspects are covered in appendices, particularly about altitude sickness, which cannot be less emphasized.

But the main strength of this book remains in the narrative that blends the real experiences and folklores. Whenever lecturing, one principle to be followed to make it interesting is to narrate stories. Presentation of the history of the peaks, lay of the land, politics and scenes of bravado are useful, but it is the interactions with locals and humour experienced on a trip that keeps the audience interested. So this book with its stories of human aspects and attractive presentation will be of interest to many.

**Harish Kapadia**
Mumbai
May 2013

## The Why, What and How of this Book

A wise man once said, 'Books are written through you, not by you' – as good a disclaimer one can conjure and one that fits particularly well in case of recreational writers like me.

My claim to writing fame so far has been an essay on 'A rainy day' in Class 7 and a one-pager on 'How I taught Physics to undergraduates' during my Berkeley stint. The writer inside me – and make no mistake, there is one inside everyone – held on to those few lines of spontaneous outburst of miraculously connected sentences for all these years. And then I started travelling in the Himalaya, Indian Himalaya to be precise (and you will catch me harping on this difference throughout the book). I travelled and I got inspired, sometimes enough to write a blog on the place I'd visited. Those few, irregular blogs caught the attention of my editor (or rather I ensured they caught her attention, she travelled with me on one of my trips you see), and the publishing house, in their infinite wisdom, felt a book on 'the other Himalaya' made sense. Just thought I should briefly share the story behind the book you are holding in your hands. And by the way, thanks for doing that; I do hope this book written through me entertains you.

Book introductions provide the writer one last chance

to influence the reader and I am going to grab this one. So here is the why, what and how of this book.

## Why another book on Himalaya?

Well, it's a book on the other Himalaya, and frankly there aren't enough. About ninety per cent of visitors to the Indian Himalaya go to the same ten per cent places year after year. This book tries to cover parts of the remaining ninety per cent and attempts to convince you, the reader, that it's very much possible to travel there, on a family holiday or as pure adventure, and does it through stories of people like you and me who have done just that.

It's these stories that form the crux of the book and differentiates it from the usual 'guidebook to the Indian Himalaya'. Of course, there is information as well, but I don't intend it to form the basis of your plans to travel on your own in the Himalaya. For that, there are genuinely good guidebooks, and I must mention the ones I have read and gained from:

- The *Outlook Traveller* books covering Uttarakhand and Himachal. Also, the monthly *Outlook Traveller* magazine, which remains the only authentic travel magazine in India, covering off-beat Himalaya in addition to the rest of the country.
- The *Driving Holidays in the Himalaya* series by Koko Singh, covering Ladakh, Zanskar, Himachal, Uttarakhand and Sikkim.
- Lonely Planet's *Trekking in the Indian Himalaya*.
- www.indiamike.com, regardless of its name, is a superb online forum where some of the best trekkers discuss

THE WHY, WHAT AND HOW OF THIS BOOK

and offer advice about almost everything related to travel in the Indian Himalaya.

This isn't a book about climbing either. I have never done any and have no qualification whatsoever to write about it. Again, there are some terrific books about climbing in the Indian Himalaya but without doubt the best of them are the 'Across Peaks & Passes' series by Harish Kapadia, covering Ladakh, Zanskar, Himachal, Garhwal, Kumaun and Sikkim. He has written about almost every climbing option (and many trekking ones as well) that currently exists, and along with his observations on the place, people and history these books are veritable encyclopaedias. When I quit my corporate job and was planning and conceptualizing CWH, I spent most of my time reading these books and they have obviously influenced the way I look at the Himalaya, its inhabitants and also the way I write.

## *What IS this book again?*

This book is a book of stories, real stories of real people who have travelled with me to the Indian Himalaya over the last five years. Weaved into the stories are facts about the people and places we visited, their past and present, and their way of life. There are ten stories from ten different regions of the Indian Himalaya, from Kashmir through Ladakh, Himachal, Uttarakhand, Sikkim and Arunachal. And since five of the ten stories are about treks we did in those regions, I can perhaps say that this book also tries to bust some of the myths and the mystique surrounding this glamorous form of walking. The doctors, homemakers, IT professionals, graphic designers, retirees, school kids, etc.

who trekked with me, most of them for the very first time, were not people you would look at and say 'now that's a fit guy/girl', but, as they too realized, on a trek fitness counts for very little. It's the ability to enjoy being in the wilderness, being away from your phone and laptop, being out of your comfort zone (yet well looked after) and most importantly the ability to feel humbled by the sheer scale of the Himalaya that matters. Strangers become friends, families strengthen their bonds, people think clearly, appreciate the small things that they take for granted and overall return with a higher respect for their abilities, and of their achievements. But it's not all hunky dory while you are actually on a trek; it's a constant challenge. People cry, shout, scream and unintentionally say and do things that they (and others) laugh at for a long time afterwards. This forms a crucial part of my stories – how people react to situations when in the mountains.

## How best to read/make sense of it?

The most important thing you should know is that the ten stories are not interconnected and therefore can be read in any sequence. You can even chose to read only about the areas that interest you or places you are planning to visit some time soon. Okay, so that out of the way, here is how I have structured the stories:

Imagine you are standing on top of a very high mountain with a very powerful zoom telescope. What you see with your naked eye: the smaller mountains, the valleys, the rivers, jungles, basically the landscape of the place then becomes '**the setting**' of my story. Now, you peer through your telescope and zoom in by 5X. You can now focus on

# CONTENTS

|  |  |  |
|---|---|---|
| | Foreword: **A few words by Harish Kapadia – the mountain man** | vii |
| | The Why, What and How of This Book | ix |
| | Prologue: **The Other Himalaya** | xvii |
| Story 1: | Kashmir – Second Chance<br>**Camping in Lidder valley and high drama in a Chaupan hut** | 1 |
| Story 2: | The Ladakh Blues, Whites and Browns<br>**The Khardung La adventure and patriotism at 4500m** | 18 |
| Story 3: | The High of Kulu Valley<br>**A path less travelled and the lost city of Thava** | 44 |
| Story 4: | Surreal Spiti<br>**The pastures of Kara and the 'friendly spirit' phenomenon** | 62 |
| Story 5: | Rupin-Supin – the Descendants of the Kauravas<br>**A village of tattooed women and surviving a Himalayan thunderstorm** | 87 |
| Story 6: | Nanda Devi – More Than a Mountain<br>**A never-ending day and the veil of the Goddess** | 109 |
| Story 7: | Darma Valley – the Land of Flying Lamas<br>**The four meadows of Nagling and the Himalayan Viagra** | 134 |

| | | |
|---|---|---|
| Story 8: | Darjeeling Hills and the Story of a Brave Girl **The day we ran for the ant-eaters** | 153 |
| Story 9: | Sikkim and the Art of Tourism **The trek cake and Nimo ke momo** | 168 |
| Story 10: | Arunachal – a Preview | 181 |
| | Epilogue: **Trekking – the Way of the Wise By Rujuta Diwekar** | 187 |

**Appendix:**

| | |
|---|---|
| Altitude Sickness | 197 |
| Common Trekking Terms | 202 |
| The Next Ten | 204 |

| | |
|---|---|
| **Acknowledgements** | 205 |

one of the valleys with a river flowing through it, its small villages with their tiny wooden huts, the flower-filled meadow and birch forest along the river, basically '**the stage**' on which the story will take place. Zoom in further, to 10X, and you can actually make out tiny figures moving along the river on a trail, ponies carrying their luggage, maybe even flashes from their cameras as they try – unsuccessfully! – to capture the ethereal landscape around them, '**the cast**'. And finally, using the super zooming magical abilities of your telescope, you zoom right into their conversations, even their thoughts and become part of '**the act**' that is playing out. This is how each of the chapters is divided – from the setting, to the stage, to the cast and finally to the story itself, or the act.

What else? There is also a '**map**'; not the type that reminds you of your geography textbook so that you want to just quickly flip the page, but hopefully a more engaging one. It's a sequence of maps actually, following the same 'zoom in' funda I explained earlier. Then there are the '**boxes**', a concept I borrowed from Rujuta's books, which allow me to write about something interesting without disturbing the flow of the story. '**Reality check**' is the space where people who are portrayed in the story get a chance to corroborate or dispute what I've written about them, and what they think of this whole big deal I am making of their holiday. And finally, each chapter is wrapped up with '**Raju, the guide**', wherein I play the ubiquitous Raju guide and dole out no-nonsense travel advice for that region. There are also references to books, guides, websites and, most importantly, to what I feel are authentic local organizations with whom you can plan your travel (assuming you will be inspired enough to travel to the region after reading my stories).

I cannot not mention the chapters that come before and after the stories. The first chapter comprises my ramblings on what I call **'the other Himalaya'**, how it's the real Himalaya and how most of the people claiming to travel in the Indian Himalaya have somehow managed to miss out on it. What is it, where is it, why is it the real deal. And the last chapter, written by **Rujuta Diwekar**, by far the best and most passionate trekker I have come across, is essentially the biggest endorsement of trekking itself. Rujuta talks about why you should follow the path of the wise when travelling in Himalaya and the physiological benefits your body reaps as a by-product of travelling in high altitudes. I can safely say that this chapter is the single-most important piece of information you can read to convince yourself to trek.

## *Parting thoughts*

All right, by now you must be itching to turn the page to the first chapter (did I tell you I am an eternal optimist), but I must hold you back for one last thing I want to share with you – writer to reader. For all the 2500 or so words I mugged up while preparing for my GRE vocabulary exam a long time back, when it came to describing the Himalaya the way my eyes saw it, I fell woefully short. Apart from 'spectacular', 'splendid', 'awesome', 'amazing', I could barely conjure up anything that does justice to the Himalaya. So please, understand this shortcoming, and read between the lines. To help you do that I have put up 'capability alerts' and directed you instead to look at the relevant photo on such and such page. The photograph is my description of the scene and the place, and though I understand it's slightly irritating to flip pages, do take a look before reading on.

And yes, the name of the book is actually the name of one of the stories and since I couldn't come up with a super cool name for the book, it made its way to the top. If you are sufficiently intrigued, jump straight to story number seven and read about the flying lama.

Lastly, I got to write this book 'luck by chance', and I am sure many of you will have better descriptions of even more spectacular places in the Indian Himalaya. I'd love to hear and read about them, and perhaps even add them in future editions of this book. You can share them with me at landofflyinglamas@gmail.com.

I can almost smell the fresh scent of the flower-filled meadows and feel the chill of the Himalayan mornings calling out from the pages ahead. I won't keep you from enjoying that any longer.

Happy reading.

**Gaurav Punj**
Mumbai
July 2013

Prologue

# The Other Himalaya

*The sacrifice of Tethys*
*Himalaya rises*
*High five*
*Trekking 101*

When I say 'the other Himalaya' it automatically implies there is more than one Himalaya. This of course is not true, there is only one Himalaya, but I mean it from the point of view of a visitor. I should perhaps call it 'the other side' of the Himalaya, a better description considering the Himalaya I refer to is beyond the lower hills. As mentioned earlier, a study on Himalayan tourism pointed out that ninety per cent of visitors to the Indian Himalaya go to only ten per cent of the places. I should add 'again and again' to this. What are those places? No prizes for guessing: hill stations and religious places (largely, the Char Dhams).

Not to take anything away from them, they became popular for a reason; they provided the perfect mix of what one wanted from a Himalayan holiday – cool climate, lots of greenery, quiet, solitude, basically a world away from the hustle and bustle of city life, and in the case of religious places, a feeling of attainment after a struggle to reach there. However, long after all of the above (except perhaps the cool climate) disappeared from their résumé, they still maintained their status as ultimate tourist hubs, primarily because the commercial interests of too many people were tied with them. Hotels, travel agents, transportation agencies, etc. that set up base there were in no mood to look beyond. Not that their clients were clamouring for change: everyone wanted (and still wants) a honeymoon in Nainital, an adventure holiday in Manali, a weekend getaway to Shimla and a super-quick pilgrimage to the Char Dhams.

Anyway, so where is this other Himalaya I speak of? It's not in the high snow-covered peaks that are great to look at but inaccessible to most, rather it's in the valleys, meadows, passes, villages, glaciers and lakes that all of us can reach and experience. Just add a few more hours to your travel from any of the hill stations and you are in this other Himalaya, suddenly realizing that all you wanted out of your holiday – in fact much more – is here. Through the stories in the next chapters we will get to know this Himalaya and the effect it has on unsuspecting visitors. But before that, a quick refresher course on the origins of the Himalaya. Trust me, I will not make it boring. In fact I am going to tell you a story, the first story there ever was.

## *The sacrifice of Tethys*

Once upon a time, a long, long time back, even before the dinosaurs roamed the earth and the earth itself didn't look the way it does now, a small piece of land rebelled and left home to see what lay beyond the sea of Tethys.

200 million years ago

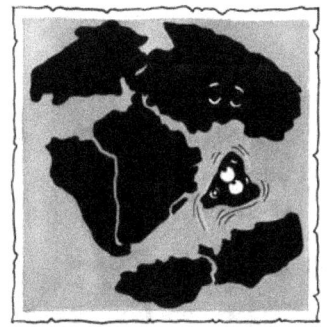
Indian subcontinent separating from Africa/Gondwana

It took her some time, but she was young and headstrong and kept at it. As she approached Tethys, she felt a pull, strong and irresistible, from Asia, and at that moment she knew that's where she had to be. Love came into existence.

120 million years ago

India approaching Tethys sea

Tethys, who had been close to Asia since she had known time, and had always believed he was hers, now realized what was inevitable. It let India plough through her to meet Asia and form a bond, strong and inseparable. From this union of India and Asia, rose Himalaya, their son, the reincarnation of Tethys.

50 million years ago – Himalaya rising from the collision (Tethys completely disappears)

25 million years ago – greater Himalaya formed

As the bond between India and Asia grew, so did Himalaya. He had all the qualities of his mother and father: strong, grand and rebellious. But most of all, like Asia, he was compassionate. As cold winds blowing down from the north ravaged India, Himalaya rose and took it upon himself to stop them, ensuring India prospered and fulfilled her destiny.

7,00,000 years ago – Himalaya rose grander. Shivalik and Gangetic plains formed

Himalaya acts as a barrier for cold winds from the north

As India became the cradle for the new order on Earth, human civilization, Himalaya fed her with water from his snows and from the monsoon clouds that would have otherwise blown over and exhausted themselves. And it continues to protect her and feed her till today. Tethys' sacrifice didn't go in vain.

Himalaya stops the monsoon clouds from blowing over

5000 years ago – the Indus valley civilization

Even today, on the windswept heights of the Himalaya, if you look specifically for it, you will find fossils of the sea creatures that lived in Tethys millions of years ago. In fact, this was the conclusive proof of the theory of how Himalaya came into being.

## *Himalaya rises*

Himalaya is the common link between Africa, the Indian subcontinent and Asia, and pretty much the whole of mankind (considering that originally all continents were part of one massive continent assembled around Africa). When it rose, it didn't rise in its entirety (covering 2500 km in length and 400 km in breadth), it did so in parts. And so we have many independent and interlinked chains of mountains (^^^^^ is a chain of mountains), which vary in height, structure, age, pretty much everything. But they are all Himalaya, and Himalaya is not one of them. Okay, I'm not trying to be philosophical; I just mean to say that these chains of mountains are collectively called the Himalaya. A few years back, just to avoid this sort of confusion, these chains of mountains were classified into four categories – lower, middle, greater and trans-Himalaya – based on certain factors, the most important of which were height and age. The following is an easy way to remember these four categories:

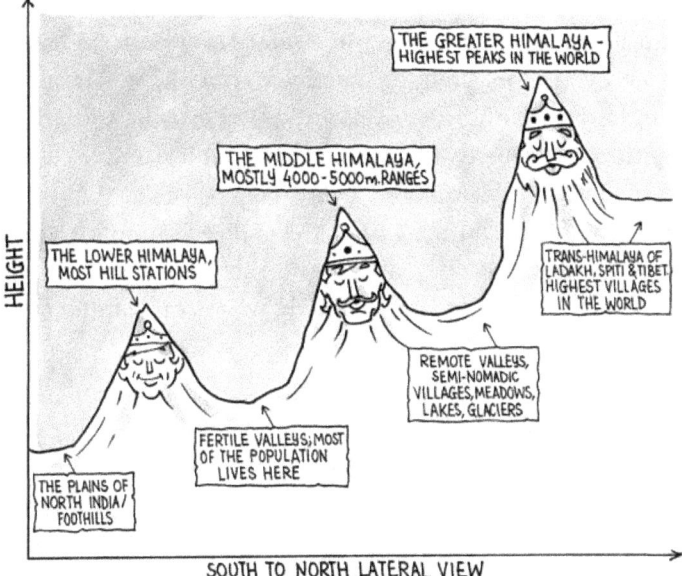

Disclaimer – This is the most rudimentary description of what is essentially 10,00,000 sq km of the most varied terrain on earth. But this is what you can think of as the 'starting point of getting to know the Himalaya'.

Okay, so I'm assuming we now have a decent enough background to revisit one of my earlier statements – drive a few hours further on from the 'hill stations', and you will be in the other Himalaya. You can now see that you will most likely be in a wooded valley with flower-filled meadows, old villages perhaps, fruit orchards for sure and invariably surrounded by high mountains on both sides. You have the choice to chill there: go for leisurely walks along the river, drive aimlessly from one village to another, pluck fruits, read a book while lying in a hammock. *Or*, you can choose to be adventurous and all and go for a section of white water rafting on the river, or an even more enjoyable activity – trekking. There are hundreds of paths that locals and shepherds have used for centuries – some easy, some not so – which will take you to meadows, glaciers and even over passes to the other side. In short, you are spoilt for choices, none of which were available to you earlier, and remember, you can do all this in relative solitude, exactly what you wanted from your holiday in the first place.

## *The high five*

Let's get a bit more specific now and talk about the Himalaya of this book – the Indian Himalaya. There are six countries through which the Himalaya passes – Afghanistan, Pakistan, India, Tibet, Nepal and Bhutan. Within India, the Himalaya passes through five states – J&K, Himachal Pradesh, Uttarakhand, Sikkim and Arunachal Pradesh. However, this is more of a geopolitical distinction and a better classification would be based on the unique regions within these states that the Himalaya passes through. Again, I think it's easier to understand this through a chart:

| Indian Himalayan States (the high five) | Regions of the other Himalaya | Some important places |
|---|---|---|
| Jammu & Kashmir | Kashmir valley | Srinagar, Pahalgam, Gulmarg, Sonmarg, Amarnath |
| | Ladakh and Zanskar | Drass, Kargil, Padum, Suru valley, Leh, Nubra valley, Pangong Tso, Chang Thang |
| Himachal Pradesh | Kulu and Parvati valleys | Manali, Naggar, Kulu, Manikaran, Shoja |
| | Chamba and Lahaul | Chamba, Bharmour, Keylong, Killar |
| | Spiti and Kinnaur | Sarahan, Sangla valley, Kalpa, Pin valley, Kaza, Tabo |
| Uttarakhand | Western Garhwal | Rupin-Supin valleys, Mori, Yamunotri, Gangotri, Kedarnath |
| | Nanda Devi and surroundings | Badrinath, Auli, Niti valley, Gwaldam, Bedni Bugyal, Munsiyari, Nanda Devi east |

|  | Eastern Kumaun | Pithoragarh, Binsar Darma, Byans and Chaudas valley |
| --- | --- | --- |
| Sikkim | Darjeeling and West Sikkim | Darjeeling, Kalimpong, Singalila ridge, Pelling, Yuksom, Barsey, Kewzing |
|  | East and North Sikkim | Neora, Rumtek, Gangtok, Lachen, Lachung, Yumthang and Thopta |
| Arunachal Pradesh | West Arunachal | Bomdilla, Dirang, Tawang |
|  | East and Central Arunachal | Ziro, Kameng valley, Miao, Namdapha |

Of course this doesn't come close to classifying all the places in the Indian Himalaya, but it is a good starting point. I have focused more on the middle, greater and trans-Himalaya, hoping you already know about the lower hills.

By design or by default, most of the other Himalaya still exists in a state that can be described as 'untouched' and I really hope that from the following stories you are inspired enough to travel there (and travel responsibly). But one last thing I want to cover in this chapter is 'trekking' – the often misunderstood key to really enjoying the mountains.

## Trekking 101

*So what exactly is a trek?* Does it involve climbing mountains, using ropes and other technical stuff? Is it for the hardcore adventurers and the really fit and young? There are as many myths surrounding trekking as there are for, let's say, avoiding carbs at night. And in both cases the culprit is misinformation. Trekking is not a technical term so it doesn't have a 'definition' as such, but for starters, you can think of it as 'a glamorous name for walking'. Of course, walking in a setting so out of the ordinary that the whole experience is lifted to a different level altogether.

From the time people settled in the Himalayan valleys, they have been rearing animals. As the shepherds, the Gujjars, etc. went higher and further in search of pastures, they found meadows full of grass where their flock could graze for the entire summer months. The paths they took, or created, were from years and years of exploring and experience. The path would usually be the easiest way from point A to point B, always close to a water source, with ideal camping sites and minimum stream crossings. When you and I walk on those paths, it's called a trek.

*And why would we want to walk on those paths?* Now this is a philosophical question and there are some 'finding yourself and getting in touch with the person inside you' type of answers to this. But to keep it simple, and believable, you should trek because it's the best way to enjoy the Himalaya. Driving through the Himalaya has its own charm, yes, but walking through it does give you a unique perspective. I am, of course, biased towards trekking, but would very strongly urge you to try it once and find the best answer to this question yourself.

*Who can trek?* If you can walk, you can trek. Since the human body was designed for activity and walking is the most basic one, so is trekking. So, age, gender, fitness levels, medical conditions are no bar. It's for everyone to enjoy and experience. As an aid, with a big 'optional' in front, you can look at the trek difficulty grade and choose accordingly.

*Trek grades:* There are no official or universally recognized grades for treks (it's just not possible), but there are some basic guidelines based on which one can grade treks.

   a) Distance walked daily – The average walking distance (better measured in time taken rather than actual kilometres) is of course the basic indicator of a trek grade.
   b) Terrain or altitude change – In addition to the altitude at which you are walking, it's the ascent and descent in a day (in other words – the sum of height gained and lost over a day) that is a better indicator of how tough the trek is.
   c) Duration – The total number of days spent trekking becomes a crucial factor. Easy trekking days spread over many days can push the perceived degree of difficulty higher.

Based on these factors, the following is one way of grading treks:

| Trek grade | Daily distance | Daily altitude change | Duration |
|---|---|---|---|
| Easy | < 4 hours | < 500m | 2-3 days |
| Medium | < 6 hours | < 800m | 3-5 days |
| Medium-hard | 6-10 hours | 800-1500m | More than 5 days |

*Note 1:* These figures are all averages and are based on data from treks I have done, and are representative of beginner as well as intermediate trekkers.

*Note 2:* A medium-hard trek could have some days that are easy or of medium level, but the overall rating is based on all three factors mentioned.

## *The horse-shit treks*

Just in case you're thinking that the other ten per cent of tourists in the Himalaya are real explorers and want to see new and

> different places, especially go on new and less crowded treks, time for a reality check. Five or six treks in the Indian Himalaya pretty much bear the brunt of this misplaced enthu. So much so that at various points of time, each one of these has been referred to as the 'horse-shit trek'. Hundreds of trekkers accompanied by hundreds of mules carrying their luggage (and sometimes the trekkers as well) trample daily on these trails. Now, I am naming some of them, but remember I have nothing against these treks, they are all superb. It's just the steadfast refusal of trekkers and trekking agencies to look beyond.
> Valley of flowers (Bhayundar valley) and Har-Ki-Dun in Garhwal
> Pindari glacier in Kumaun
> Beas Kund in Himachal
> Padum-Darcha and Markha valley in Ladakh
> Give them a break people, you will not miss out on anything if you go on other treks, in fact, you will only gain from the uncorrupted trails, people and scenery.
> Note: Harish Kapadia's upcoming book is a collection of treks he did in the Indian Himalaya, and there are 120 treks listed in there.

*A typical trekking day*: It really is a big mystery for every first-time trekker. I remember the first time I trekked, I was shocked at how different reality was from what I'd imagined. So here goes, a typical day on a trek, from my perspective of course:

The day starts very early, sometimes as early as 5 a.m., but usually by 6 a.m. The reason being the settled weather conditions in the first half of the day. You brush your teeth, answer nature's call (amidst nature or in a dry pit toilet covered by a toilet tent but away from a water source) and get ready for a heavy breakfast of aloo parantha, toast with peanut butter and jam, eggs, cereal, milk, chai, coffee, etc. Stretch and start walking with your day pack. Porters and mules will carry the luggage and a guide will accompany you, describing the terrain through which you are passing. Everyone walks at his/her own pace and there is no hurry to finish the day's walk in any specific time period. After a couple of hours, stop and have a portion of the packed lunch, probably a boiled potato, juice, egg and parantha or puri bhaji. You will also carry your own snacks – peanuts, dry fruit, chocolates, etc. The idea is to eat small meals throughout the walk. Finish the day's walk by afternoon and do cool down stretches on reaching the campsite. The cook will prepare a hot meal or evening snacks of pakoras with tea, etc. depending on what time you finish. Chill for the rest of the day. Play cards or sleep or read as you please. The day is wrapped up by a heavy hot dinner by 7 p.m. After dinner, a round of gossip, games or songs and off to sleep by 9 p.m. latest.

*Trek preparation*: Can safely divide this into mental and physical conditioning.

Mental preparation: The most important characteristic required for trekking is a sound temperament. I would any day rate it higher than physical fitness. By its very nature, trekking is an unpredictable activity. You are at the mercy of nature and have to be prepared for everything: fickle weather (can be very sunny, then windy, then rainy and sunny again, all in less than thirty minutes) and pre-conceived notions. The thing to know (and understand) is that no matter how easy the trek grade, you are always going to be out of your comfort zone. Once you make peace with this, trust me, you will fall head over heels (figuratively only) for trekking.

Physical preparation: If it's an easy or medium grade

trek, basic fitness levels, that is, an ability to walk (and enjoy it) is all that you need. Of course if you are working out, running or any form of exercise, it will surely make trekking effortless and more enjoyable. For hard treks, it's perhaps better to be prepared, especially by following a well-rounded training programme. This will usually be a mix of strength training, cardio-respiratory fitness and core strength and balancing.

And just before you get pakaoed from all the gyan, let me wrap up the chapter with the **top five trekking quirks** – remember, you read them here first:

1. Trekkers have wild mood swings. They cry, they sulk, they scream, they exult, they hug, they laugh like they have never laughed before, the whole jingbang. You can apply your own expertise in psychology to explain this but I think they are just overwhelmed.

2. Never listen to a returning trekker. They will massively exaggerate the difficulty of the trek and will directly/indirectly imply that while they have been able to finish it, you don't stand a chance. They feel invincible and you are a mere mortal now.

3. When on a trek, existence is reduced to the bare basics, things that are essential but ignored in our daily lives. For example, it's pretty common on a trek to have hour-long discussions (passionate ones, too) on the colour, consistency and smell of your potty. Arguments break out over who snores the most or people share their deepest secrets about how often they actually bathe, brush, etc. back home.

4. Men whine much more than women while trekking. Oh boy, I have put this in writing now, so no going back, bring on the anti-generalization brigade. But seriously, women are much more flexible in mind, much more adventurous, and believe it or not, much stronger.
5. If someone says they do eco-friendly trekking, slap them; okay, at least laugh to their face. Are you the type to litter while walking at home or outside on the streets or break rules for fun? If not, you won't do that on a trek either, right? So why should someone else get the credit for your good habits. Trekking by default is an eco-friendly activity; you can only make it 'non-eco' by being inconsiderate.

Story 1

# Kashmir – the Second Chance

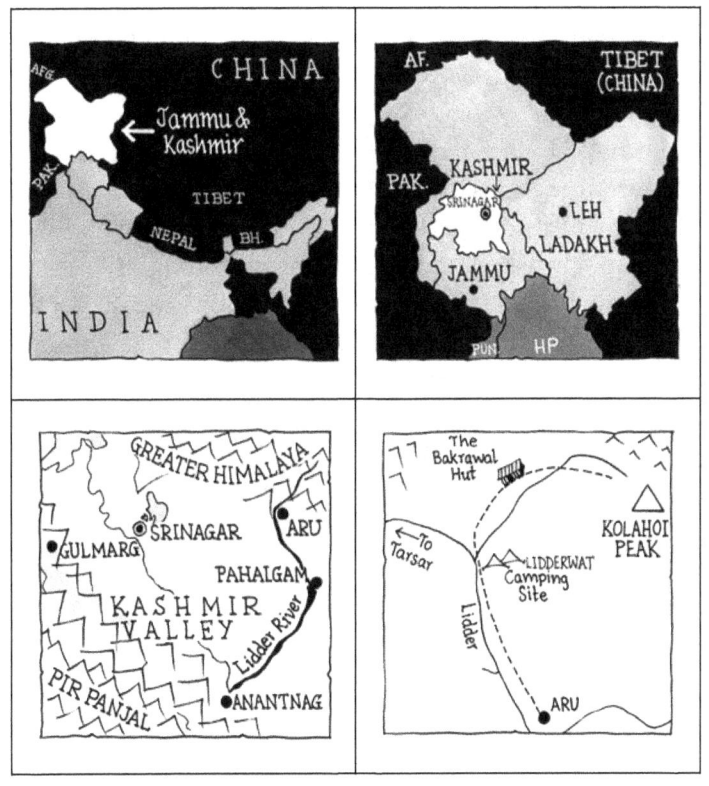

Hand-drawn maps for representation purposes only. Not to scale.

## *The setting*

There is something special about Kashmir, and you come face-to-face with this fact the moment the plane starts its descent into Srinagar. The valley springs out from the clutches of the high, windswept mountains of the Pir Panjal range and opens up in kilometre-wide green opulence, interspersed with log huts, Chinar trees and the Jhelum. Yes, you can see all this from the window of your airplane. It's an unusually wide valley, wider than any in the Indian Himalaya, and that, more than anything else, makes it what it is.

I have been going to Kashmir every year since 2006 and have noticed the gradual thawing of the decades' long winter, of tensions and resentments against whomsoever they were meant. Earlier, as soon as you left the airport, you could sense the tension throbbing through the roads, the silent glares of the locals and the automatic rifles of the army men posted every hundred metres. To be honest, I never really felt at ease while in Srinagar, though I wanted to, badly.

From the Lal Chowk bomb blast of 2006 while we were having lunch just a block away, and the slogans of 'Azaadi, azaadi…' chanted coldly in 2007, to the 'no room available in entire Srinagar' situation in 2011, it has been a steady progress towards the oft-quoted 'golden era of Kashmir tourism' which was fuelled by the enterprising Kashmiri and the Hindi movie industry. It still has some way to go; the tourism infrastructure needs to catch up with the rest of the Himalayan states; but it is progress nonetheless.

Pahalgam is 100 km southwest of Srinagar and is one of the towns in the holy trinity of Kashmir tourism, Gulmarg and Sonmarg being the other two. Don't miss the ruins at Avantipur, just outside Srinagar, as you drive towards the town with two names, Anantnag and Islamabad, before catching up with the Lidder river and then following it all the way to Pahalgam. From there, continue along the Lidder for 15 km and you'll reach the quintessential Kashmiri village of Aru.

## *The stage*

Aru is a village set around a huge meadow with a small stream flowing through it. There are log huts set up by the tourism department right in the middle, occupying the best location, but they weren't functional when we visited. On the periphery are a few more guesthouses, and we stayed in one of them, the only guests in Aru. It was 2008 and the valley was just about recovering from the long lull and tourists were starting to trickle in. Our guesthouse owner, though, acted as if we had disturbed his restful times staying alone in this idyllic village. An attitude not too different from a few other locals we encountered on our trip.

We were in Aru because we were planning to do a short trek that starts from there, goes along the Lidder stream to Lidderwat and further towards the snout of the Kolahoi glacier. In its prime, tourism-wise, Kashmir was a magnet unlike any for trekkers, and the crown jewel was this trek and its off-shoots. It was on this trek that three trekkers were abducted and killed in 1989, in a chilling and definitive end to the golden era. Historic significance was not on our mind however when we chose the trek, it was the fact that it's easy, short and stunningly beautiful. Our contacts in Kashmir had assured us of its safety, and here we were.

Lidder valley is also home to the semi-nomadic tribes of Gujjars, Chaupans and Bakrawals, herders of cattle, sheep and goats respectively. An entirely unique set of people. They have been leading the same way of life for ages now; they don't recognize state borders and, most intriguingly, they don't give a damn about anybody. Very similar in their looks, traditions and attitude, but make the mistake of mixing up one for the other and they will not waste a moment in correcting you, sternly of course. They live a semi-nomadic life with separate winter and summer homes. The summer abode is more a temporary shelter made of rocks high up in the mountains. But cosy nonetheless. And into one such hut we stumbled.

## *The cast*

In order of appearance: Javed, our voluble guide for the trek, his assistant Nadeem, a Gujjar couple, the open-air schoolteacher, and the two Chaupan women. Our group included Rujuta, her father, Bhavana, a hardcore IT professional, Zahir, a hardcore ad guy, and me.

## *The act: Camping in Lidder valley and high drama in a Chaupan hut*

'Good morning sirs and madams, I Javed, guide for Lidder valley trek,' Javed introduced himself in the same forced accented English that everyone in the tourism industry here seems to have picked up from God knows where. It was an effort to get Javed to speak to us in Hindi and took us almost a day. 'And where are the cook and horseman?' I asked. 'Me only is everything,' came the reply wrapped in a sheepish smile. 'Don't worry.'

Surprisingly, we *weren't* worried. We were so taken in by the indescribable beauty of Aru, and by all indicators, it would only get better on the trek. So with our guide-cum-cook-cum-horseman, two ponies and an assistant (small mercies), we started the walk from the village market. 'Just small climb, then straight all day,' was Javed's description of the first day's trek. It turned out to be factually correct, but boy, there was so much more.

The initial climb took us to the top of a knoll overlooking Aru, which was guarded by a couple of army men, and it gave us a good excuse to catch our breath. We said hello to the jawans and told them we were going for a trek. 'Kyon aaye ho idhar marne,' was the deadpan response. They're just bored and homesick, we decided and moved on. We immediately entered a thick forest of pine and deodar and began walking on a well-defined path. Javed and his small gang had gone ahead to pitch the camp and all we had to do was walk along the trail at our own pace. Soon we came across the first of many interesting scenes we would be witness to through the trek. It was a Gujjar couple with their month-old baby, dressed in all their traditional glory, walking purposefully towards Aru. 'Her vaccination for this month is due,' the mother told us with a shy smile, but matter-of-factly. I love the Gujjars for the way they have assimilated 'modernity' while leading a, what appears to be, primitive lifestyle. At that moment however these thoughts were not in our mind, we were too busy admiring the baby and her attire. Will let the picture do the talking. It's on page i in the inserts.

Soon we were out of the forest and in the wide, open Lidder valley. THE Lidder valley, I should say. Let's use our imagination a bit now. You are looking from top and can see tiny figures emerging from the forest into wide grassy grounds, gently sloping down. To their left is a stream, crystal clear, bubbly, azure blue, 15-20 feet wide, with more pastures on the other bank sloping up steeply, this time to a patch of deodar at the base of a huge mountain. Miniature sheep, goat and other cattle, as seen from your high perch, are grazing rather lazily on the abundant grass on both banks. You see the tiny dots stop in their track, looking all around them, with their mouths open, you can very well assume, and then there is a flurry of flashes, the memory cards of their cameras fast filling up in a futile attempt to capture what their eyes can see. One of them even walks to the bank of the river, lies down on his stomach in a weird position and flashes away.

Giving up on trying to capture the scale of the valley, its greenery, and in the case of Zahir, the twists of the Lidder, we strolled on. The camp was just a couple of kilometres away and we had the whole day. You know how we use the term 'surreal' so frivolously sometimes? But what we saw next truly did do justice to the term. On the slopes, lush with grass, were about twenty children seated in five rows. They were in some sort of a school uniform, and facing them, seated on a chair, was a man. They all looked at us with the same amusement as we looked at them. It lasted for a few seconds or so and was soon replaced with broad smiles on both sides. We spoke to the man and found out what it was: a summer school for the Gujjar, Bakrawal and Chaupan children sponsored by the government. The funding included the uniforms, books, lunch and a full-time teacher. The rows represented grades I to V. The kids seemed to enjoy reading the beautifully designed and illustrated textbooks, and the teacher, Bilal, was kind and gentle, and didn't think much of his daily walk to Aru. Overall, it was a feel good picture government brochures would kill for. The photograph is on page i in the inserts.

As Baba took Sir's interview, we spoke briefly to the kids, clicked some pix and waved our goodbye, it was a school in session after all and one shouldn't disturb them for long. Also, we were hungry. We reached our camp where two huge tents, straight out of the 1980s, had been pitched on the grassy bank of the river. Not much of trekking has been happening here and the equipment was just a reflection of that. One was a kitchen/sleeping tent for Javed and his assistant and the other was where all five of us would sleep.

The camp had been set up at Lidderwat, and just ahead were settlements of Chaupans and Bakrawals. It was no doubt an exceptionally pretty site, but we decided to eat first and look around later. Javed was not in the mess tent however, but soon we could hear his shouts as he appeared on the scene, wildly chasing one of the ponies, which he eventually managed to catch and tie to a boulder. Panting, he came up to us and complained, 'Lunch is ready, why you so late, I got bored.'

Lunch was, to put it mildly, a not very tasty concoction of rice and sabzi, but Javed insisted it was Kashmiri pulao and coerced us into praising his cooking skills. We had to give it to the man for his sheer enthusiasm and entertainment quotient though. He laughed loudly at his stupidest jokes, sulked majorly if we didn't praise his cooking or didn't include him in our kitchen tent conversations, chased ponies every few hours like a crazed man and 24x7 pretended to be a pro guide-cum-cook-cum-horseman. But behind the eccentric persona he projected was a practical man, a man who has suffered the hardships of a very long proxy war, and who now wants to work hard and make the most of the second chance he has got. We glimpsed that Javed once in a while, especially when he would make statements like, 'Why does everyone ask us if we want India or Pakistan; we just want tourists.' And it endeared him to us.

## *A short history of Kashmir*

It would need many volumes to cover Kashmir's history in its entirety, so this is barely a glimpse of the 'glimpse of a short history of Kashmir'.

| Time period | Dominant religions | To be noted… |
| --- | --- | --- |

| Earliest – 3000 BC to 1350 AD | Hinduism Buddhism | In mythology, **Kashyapa rishi** drained the Kashmir valley and settled Brahmins there. **Ashoka** established the city of Srinagar in 300 BC and introduced Buddhism to the region. Hinduism resurged in about 800 AD under the Karkota dynasty. |
|---|---|---|
| Middle – 1350 AD to 1819 AD | Islam | Initially under the **Shah Mir** dynasty, Islam gradually spread and became dominant with Persian replacing Sanskrit as the official language by 1550 AD. Then came Mughals, first indirectly, and then directly ruling Kashmir under **Akbar** from 1589 AD. |
| Latest – 1819 AD to 1947 AD | Islam under Sikh rule | In 1819 AD came the Sikhs under **Ranjit Singh** and ruled a state with 77% Muslim and 20% Hindu subjects. This rule lasted till Hari Singh in 1947. |

It was warm in the tent and we slept soundly. The next day was a rather long one; we were to walk as close to the Kolahoi glacier as we could and then return to Lidderwat and our camp. It was also a day when we would gain some height, and perhaps climb till 3200m. After breakfast, Baba came up to me and told me he felt like returning as he 'can't shit in the open'. We didn't have toilet tents on this trip, so the business was to be done behind a rock or a tree. Well, not much to argue there, although I had a feeling he was not yet done with interviewing Bilal and just wanted more time with him. Javed offered to walk him back to Aru and to the guesthouse there, while we went ahead with Nadeem.

We started soon and after crossing the Lidder over a log bridge, caught the trail going up. All through we could see Gujjar, Chaupan and Bakrawal settlements. These were largely temporary huts made of loose stones and wood, set at a distance of about twenty feet or so from each other, and built into the slope of the mountains such that if one looked from the top, they just merged in with the terrain, very much like military bunkers. Soon we reached the point from where the trail bifurcates, one towards the Kolahoi glacier, the other towards Tarsar lake. There were dense forests of birch (bhoj patra), the highest Himalayan tree, growing as they always do, almost perpendicular to the steep slopes. Our trail now passed through the terminal moraine of Kolahoi glacier, and was therefore more rocky and harsh. There were no trees any longer, the sun was sharp and the altitude began to have an effect on us. Bhavana, who had literally been bouncing ahead in the morning, was the first casualty. She sat on a rock and refused to move, her head in her hands.

She had begun to display signs of, what would be known on our future treks as, the 3000-metre Bhavana syndrome. She got up from the rock, swerved wildly and scampered towards the nearest hut, with us following fast behind her. As soon as she reached the hut, a Chaupan woman, the inhabitant of that hut, emerged to enquire what we wanted. Ignoring her welcome, Bhavana went inside and made herself comfortable on her bed. Let's call it, err, the true survivor's instinct. While Bhavana lay on her bed, a scene not so different from Ram-Bharat milap was being played outside. The Chaupan woman greeted all of us with a big smile, turned to Rujuta and hugged her so tightly and for so long, it almost brought tears to the eyes of the unflappable Konkanastha brahmin. Damn, they even looked alike (photograph on page ii in the inserts).

She then took us inside her hut, which was homely, warm, comfortable, spacious – things one would not have imagined looking at it from the outside. By now Bhavana had started crying, which made us very concerned at first, but we quickly realized we had to let her be. The Chaupan woman, whose name we never asked, as she never asked ours, communicated in her broken Hindi that she was making something special for herself and us. A younger Chaupan woman, from the neighbouring hut, joined us along with her six-month-old baby; she didn't want to be left out of all the fun.

If someone had walked into the hut at that time, this is the scene he/she would have witnessed: on the left, the Chaupan woman leaning over her chullah, making some special concoction while beaming at Rujuta, who was seated next to her. Behind them, on the gadda on the floor was Bhavana, sobbing; at her feet was Zahir, sitting cross-legged, with his eyes closed, determination on his face and hands on Bhavana's feet, 'healing' her with his newly learnt Reiki; and by his side, the other Chaupan woman with her baby on her lap, trying to make conversation with me about Mumbai and weather. Don't forget, we were on the moraine of the Kolahoi glacier, in a small, semi-permanent shelter, surrounded by mountains so high and a valley so wide, we really couldn't have been more insignificant.

Soon enough, the magic potion was ready and it turned out to be the best kahwa we have tasted till date. It was a perfect blend of almonds, cardamom, cinnamon, cloves, black pepper and, most importantly, kesar. I can't really say if it was the kahwa or the Reiki, but Bhavana started feeling better and even got up for a while. The younger Chaupan woman was by now playing with Zahir's SLR, specifically the lens. Zahir tried telling her to not put her fingerprints on the lens, but in vain. What's the big deal, was her expression. All this while, her baby was kicking and laughing loudly. Suddenly he started to roll out of her lap and was about to fall face first to the ground. We all screamed in unison, 'Arre arre, dekho', and heroically lunged forward to protect him. The woman nonchalantly pulled him back on her lap, looked at our worried faces with a smile and said, 'Go toh go.'

We stared with open mouths, the lady's super-quick reflexes and the associated coolness yet to sink in, when, I could have sworn, the baby winked at us. 'Gotcha,' he was probably thinking. 'Go toh go,' we repeated to ourselves, almost like a mantra, hoping we could assimilate this lesson taught by the Chaupan woman. Zahir even put it into practice immediately and let go of his attempts to save his camera lens. We also let go of Bhavana and decided to let her rest while we walked ahead towards the glacier.

\* \* \*

## *Reality check*

**Bhavana Mehta**
**Ex-IT guru and now a fashion designer**

*I don't know what hit me that day. A throbbing headache, nausea, extreme tiredness, wanting to cry, not wanting to walk anymore... Luckily there was a hut close by and I just knew I had to go in. The lady in the hut welcomed us with a very warm smile. I barged in and found a place where I could lie down, forgetting all formalities; it was wonderfully warm and cosy inside. She made kahwa, which I love, and perhaps it helped me fall asleep. When I woke up there was no one in the hut. My friends have deserted me, was my first reaction. How could they, just because I slept? The Chaupan lady was there however, ever smiling, and told me they would be back soon. She asked me if I needed a mule to ride down, but I figured it would be better to keep my feet on the ground. GP and the others returned soon and we started our walk back. When we reached camp, Rujuta lay down flat on the grassy slope and started rolling down. She asked me to do the same and experience how it feels. It felt awesome; all my aches and pains had disappeared by then.*

* * *

We walked for about twenty minutes, but the glacier had receded too far away and could not have been reached for another two hours, so we just took in the stunning Kolahoi peak looming in front and returned to fetch Bhavana. We debated whether to give any 'tip' to the woman – it's hard to let go of bad habits –but wisely decided against it; they looked so proud and content, what indeed could we give them. Warm goodbyes were said, some more hugging took place and with a still stuttering Bhavana we started our journey back.

We walked in a much more relaxed fashion on the way back, which btw, always happens. The tension of having to reach somewhere and the thought of the return journey keeps you strung up and the walk back is when you actually enjoy the scenery and observe all the wonderful things on a trek. And so we saw a snow patch close by, just off the trail, and decided to walk up to it. I guess we are all competitive to various degrees and it's difficult at such moments to differentiate between the urge to explore and the need to prove something. Anyway, leaving Bhavana to rest on a rock (collapsed on a rock, I should say; it was still above 3000m), and me to my camera, which in such situations acts as a good excuse to not go scampering up steep slopes, Rujuta and Zahir started walking towards the snow. They were soon joined by couple of Gujjar men and I could hear them all laughing while briskly walking up. Not for long though. The pace slowed down, then the 'hands on knees' posture we all know so well, some longing glances back toward us, a discussion and the return march.

In no time we were back on the grassy meadows, which after a day on loose rock felt even more inviting, and we celebrated by doing a 'roll down the slope' routine, one by one, including the miraculously recovered Bhavana (and here is proof on page ii in the inserts).

It was getting late and we knew Javed would give us a tough time about boring him, which he did, to perfection: the sulking face, hurt tone, all of it was there. He soon cheered up though; it was time for his favourite chore – cooking dinner. Bhavana, after her 3000m syndrome, was in her element and took it upon herself to 'assist' Javed, which soon became 'instruct' Javed. 'Yeh kya kiya?', 'Namak kam daalo', and Javed was on the brink of leaving us and going back. We had to diplomatically resolve this situation and ensure we had something to eat that night. Which by the way, was a moonlit night unlike any we had seen. The rustling Lidder, the silhouettes of our ponies grazing on the banks, the snow-covered peaks and a full moon in the sky. Did someone say something about Kashmir being a paradise? He was right.

The return trek to Aru was uneventful and we thoroughly enjoyed the scenery, knowing very well how lucky we were to get a chance to see Kashmir like this. A chance we had felt we might never get, a chance which not just us, an entire generation felt was denied to them, a chance which Javed never stopped dreaming about. For all of us, Javed and Kashmir, this is a second chance and we must make the most of it.

* * *

## Raju, the Guide
*Short mein bole toh, Kashmir is back. Just go there, anytime.*

## More reading
Some books and guides that are easily available and which I have managed to read and gained from (Note – since 1989, almost no travel guide covers Kashmir, which will change soon of course):

| Title | Category | Author | Remarks |
|---|---|---|---|
| *Kashmir As It Was* (1908) | History and exploration | Francis Younghusband | A comprehensive book on Kashmir by one of the empire's best explorers. |
| *Travels in Kashmir* (1989) | Travelogue / history | Brigid Keenan | A non-academic, easy to read history of travel, religion and arts in Kashmir. |
| Lonely Planet *Kashmir, Ladakh & Zanskar* (1989) | Guidebook | Margaret and Rolf Schettler | It's out of print right now, but check out travel bookshops – you might get lucky. |
| *Eighty-three Days: The Story of a Frozen River* (2000) | Memoir | Dr S.N. Dhar | The author was taken hostage in 1992. This is one of the few inside accounts of those times. |

## What else to do in Kashmir
*Trekking* – The region between Pahalgam and Sonmarg has some really good, easy treks and they are all open now for tourists. And whenever restrictions are lifted from

Kishtwar, don't wait a day to trek there – it's the ultimate destination.

*Skiing* – The global consensus is that Gulmarg has some of the best skiing slopes, and now that it has good places to stay, ski lifts and a wonderful gandola (highest in the world), no reason not to go there in winter.

*Chilling out* – Try Srinagar in autumn or early spring and you will never want to be anywhere else. It has places to stay to suit all budgets.

## Point to be noted

The houseboats have fallen out of favour as they have suffered the most from the long absence of tourists. They're not clean and are constantly frequented by touts trying to sell you something. But there is hope that they will soon recover as the romance of staying on the Dal lake and seeing the sun rise or set is unbeatable. For now, stay at the more popular ones, even if it means having to spend a little more.

## Local service providers

Unfortunately, it's tough to recommend a local trekking agency, they are still in the process of getting better, but in Pahalgam you can get in touch with the Jawahar Institute of Mountaineering and Winter Sports for help with your trek. www.jawaharinstitutepahalgam.com.

Javed didn't have a contact number at that point of time, or perhaps I lost it, but I am hopeful I will find him soon enough; he'll probably be taking pilgrims on his pony to Amarnath. But I can recommend a local guide in Gulmarg who is genuine and resourceful and helps with your stay, trekking, skiing, etc. Nisar Bhai: 9906829949.

Story 2

# The Ladakh Blues, Whites and Browns

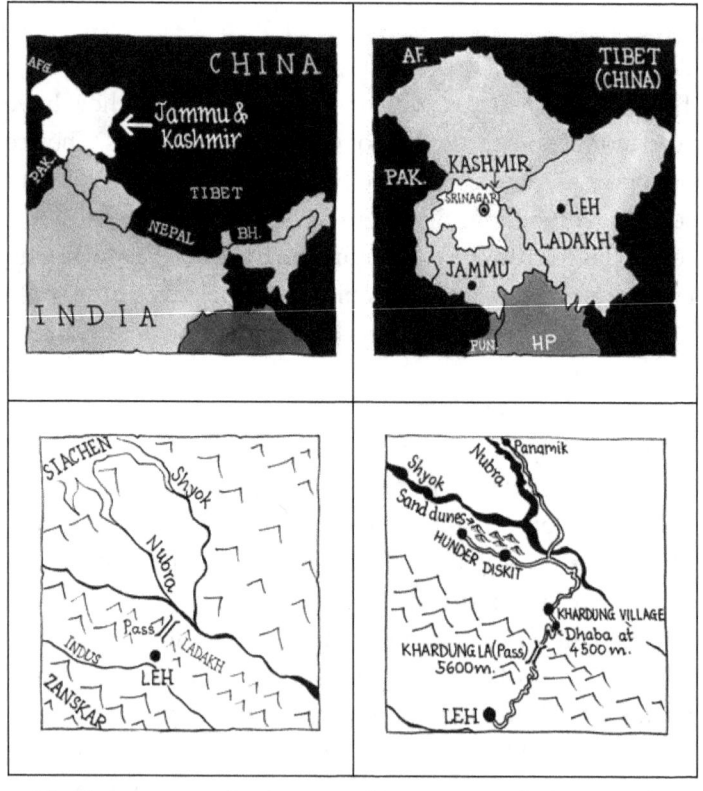

Hand-drawn maps for representation purposes only. Not to scale.

## *The setting*

Much before the Bajaj Avenger rode through its dusty lands and the rider 'forgave us all', before 3 *Idiots* put Pangong Tso on the national must-see list and increased the GDP of Ladakh by twenty-five per cent, and before a freak cloudburst made people realize that Leh is no ordinary hill station, Ladakh had captured the imagination of many a wanderer. It was THE place to go to if you were looking to travel to 'discover what life is' and other such pseudo-intellectual pursuits, as people sought answers in its starkness. But I am still talking about the last decade; let's go back a bit more. In the '80s and '90s it was the snow leopard that put Ladakh on the conservation and documentary map. Otherwise not much happened there from 1949 onwards when the Chinese closed the border trade between Nubra and Sinkiang. But before that, boy, it was rocking.

Leh, the largest town in Ladakh, happened to be conveniently located on one of the busiest junctions on the world's greatest and oldest trading routes, collectively called the Silk Route (ah, whoever came up with that name must have been a die-hard romantic). 'The cross-roads of high Asia,' as Janet Rizvi called it in her book with the same title, was perhaps the world's first and truly global village, with traders from all over, including Turkestan, Tibet, Punjab, Kashmir and Baltistan, always present in its inns, drinking chang one would imagine, and resting their tired limbs. Ladakhis themselves weren't much of traders however, apart from some in the border areas, and prospered from the trade route by levying taxes on goods passing through their land. In the 19th century, an additional, although minor, activity led to the infusion of some more cash: adventure tourism.

Yes. As per Arthur Neves' *The Tourist's Guide to Kashmir, Ladakh and Skardo*, first published in 1911, there were agencies set up for 'trekking, fishing, etc.' as early as the 19th century (another first I would presume). I didn't do any major research for this – it's common knowledge and is even on Wikipedia. The point I am making is that Ladakh always had this 'pull'; it might have lost it temporarily for a few decades, but it's back now, stronger than ever.

A quick word on the most fascinating aspect of Ladakh: Buddhism. As one travels from Kashmir to Ladakh, not only does the terrain change, so do the people and the culture and religion they follow. From Kashmiri Islam, it shifts to the Dard culture (a unique mixture of Islam and Buddhist practices) of Kargil and Suru valley and then, from Mulbek onwards, to the Tibetan Buddhism of Ladakh and upper Zanskar.

Spiti in Himachal also has a similar transformation from Hinduism to Buddhism. Between Ladakh and Spiti, they have managed to retain and, in many ways, add to this form of Buddhism, and are perhaps the last surviving pure Tibetan Buddhism centres.

For the uninitiated, Buddhism spread from India to Tibet (in addition to many other places) around 7th century AD, and a couple of centuries later came back from there to Ladakh and Spiti, in a modified version called Tibetan Buddhism (the combination of Buddhism with the native Bon religion of Tibet, or 'nature worship').

## The stage

From Leh, you can see two prominent chains of mountains, the Ladakh range to the north and Zanskar towards the south. Between these two flows the Indus, the mighty river that predates even the Himalaya. One can cross over either of these two ranges on motorable roads, amongst the highest in the world. And in the case of the Ladakh range, after crossing the Khardung La, one reaches the greenest valley in Ladakh – the Nubra valley. Two rivers, Nubra and Shyok, flow through it and these combined with the lower altitude make it conducive for agriculture. Paradoxically, this is also the valley with the only sand dunes in Ladakh.

Vagaries of nature aside, it came into prominence recently because through it passes the road to the Siachen glacier and the northernmost tip of India. Locals, so cut off from the world for ages, have still not been able to come to terms with the valley's status as one of Ladakh's holy tourist trinity, along with Pangong lake and Leh town.

## The cast

Indian and foreign tourists stranded in the Nubra valley, the dhaba family, our two drivers Tashi and Sonam, and our group of eight.

## The act: The Khardung La adventure and patriotism at 4500m

'Will there be snow on the top?' 'Yes, more than you can handle,' I replied, without realizing how true these words were going to be. We had just started climbing up towards the Khardung La from the Leh side. It was 8 a.m., the air was absolutely still, the sky a deep blue, a monastery on a hill was lit up by the sun, and the Indus was snaking its way through the high plateau in the distance, in other words, a typical morning in Ladakh. We were in two cars, the eight of us, and by now felt like veterans of the Ladakhi roads with around 500 km under our belt since we'd started from Srinagar. But this was the highest we would go on this trip, on any trip ever, and the excitement levels were more than 5600m high. Over dinner the previous night, we had spoken about our strategy for the world's highest motorable road – while going to Nubra, spend as little time as possible on the top, leave all the fun, i.e. snow fights, photographs, souvenirs, etc. for the way back. Logic: more time to acclimatize.

All well and good was the general mood as we started gaining height, fast. We passed a bunch of cyclists, all foreigners, on their way up, really struggling but persevering. The usual debate on how all foreigners are so fit and Indians aren't ensued and I contributed with my well-practised line: 'Not all foreigners are fit; only the fit ones come here to do such hardcore activities.'

It had started getting cold, and we rolled up the car windows, put on an extra sweater, cap and snuggled closer to each other. 'Keep sipping water,' I gently reminded everyone, and they did so obediently. The group surely had a sense of occasion and they knew where they were. My job is easy, I thought to myself.

We were now above 4500m and soon enough snow appeared on the side of the road and as usual the sight excited everyone. The car was stopped and photographs clicked, the cold and acclimatization forgotten for the time being. We could also see fresh footprints of an animal, identified by our driver, Tashi, as blue sheep; it must have scampered up the slope on hearing our vehicle approaching. It was windy and that ensured that no one could stay out for long, so we soon started the drive up.

We crossed South Pullu, an army checkpoint (and a place to pee), and now were on the final climb to the top.

## *The Khardung La adventure*

In an exhibition of how quickly the weather changes in the Himalaya, especially at such high altitudes, a factor most recreational tourists to Ladakh have still not understood, the wind brought with itself fast moving clouds. Within no time, less than ten minutes to be precise, the scene had changed: sunlight replaced with low visibility, crisp air with moisture, Tashi's whistling with his intense gaze fixed to the top of the pass, excited chatter in the car with tense silence. The Khardung La adventure had begun.

It wasn't raining but Tashi had to use his wipers anyway to clear the moisture build up on the windscreen. 'Have you ever seen snow fall?' I asked Arzoo. She nodded, though her eyes were focused on the road ahead, like everyone else in the car, silently backing Tashi. 'And a snowstorm?' This got her to abandon Tashi for a moment and look at me with a mixture of thrill and apprehension, I guess, but which somehow manifested itself as an angry expression. 'Not that I am saying there will be a snowstorm. July and August is not the time for snowstorms, don't worry,' I blurted quickly before the others turned on me too, and tried to change the subject by asking Tashi, 'How much more time to the top?' An uncharacteristically sombre Tashi replied with a 'Mausam pe hai sir, phas bhi sakte hain.' And we were well and truly psyched.

The weather gods must have decided not to fuel our apprehensions any longer, and there it was, the snowflakes on the windscreen, the first place they are always noticed. As the wipers struggled to clear the snow and the car slowed down, we realized the snowfall hadn't just started; we had only entered the area where it had been snowing already. There was snow on the road and as we drove cautiously over the tracks made by cars ahead of us, we knew it would take a long time to cover these last 2-3 km to the top. And soon enough, there was the first skid, a shriek, tentative laughter, change of gears and inaudible cursing. 'Bhaiya sambhal ke,' one of us offered this useless advice to an already tense Tashi, and he smartly ignored it. It's not uncommon for them to drive through snow when going up to or down from Khardung La.

The snowfall was steady and the entire scene was, well, it's tough to describe when the only colour you see everywhere is white. The mountain ranges, which now appeared to be lower than us, were covered in a fresh layer of snow, snowflakes were falling in slow motion in the valley below, the road ahead was white, and it all felt really cold. On cue, the car gave a jerk and Tashi brought it to a stop before declaring, 'Dhakka marna padega, too slippery.'

We all got out quite happily: it was too much to sit in a skidding car. Some of us pushed the car and some walked along on the frozen road (photograph on page iii in the inserts). A couple of hundred metres further we turned a bend and there it was, the top. More importantly, a cafeteria run by the army.

Quite a few cars were parked there and the cafeteria was bustling with activity. The army was offering hot kahwa to everyone, and we also had the choice of buying a cup of tea, coffee, a plate of samosa or Maggi. However precarious your situation might be, it's amazing how hot food and a cup of tea can make you feel better. We were at 5600m, really really high by any standard, there was a snowstorm outside, cars couldn't drive us out of there, and here we were, talking animatedly about the amazing marketing and reach of instant noodles.

The altitude though had the final say and when the forced break extended for more than an hour, quite a few people in the cafeteria started feeling it. An altitude-induced headache is quite different from the common one. For starters, it is always accompanied by at least two or three of its sidekicks, breathlessness and dizziness being the prominent ones. And because you're suffering from it at a place far away and vastly different from your home, it gets exaggerated in your mind. Lastly, there is so much conflicting information on what caused it and how to deal with it, that it can be overwhelming. Allow me to promote one of the appendices in this book (page 203): From my travels, from listening to people's experiences and from research, books, articles on the subject, I have collated all that you need to know and understand about altitude sickness.

Anyhow, we are still at the top of Khardung La, the snow has stopped falling, but the army hasn't given the green signal for vehicles to cross over, even though their supplies of hot drinks and snacks are almost over. 'Checking the roads, sir,' Tashi told us. He and all the other drivers were standing outside in the open, laughing out loud, pulling each other's leg, things they would do if they were waiting outside a shaadi party in Delhi. We envied them their immunity towards the cold and altitude, conveniently forgetting that this is their home, their way of life.

'Chalo sir,' Tashi finally came inside to call us, and we literally jumped from our chairs, so willing now to sit in the same car we'd been desperate to get out of an hour and a half back. The high Himalayan weather reinforced its unpredictable nature by showering us with bright, warm sunlight and blue skies with fast moving clouds, this time moving away from each other.

We were soon on the other side of the Khardung La where the Nubra valley lies. It's the northern side, so there was much more snow here and the asphalt road snaking through the snow provided for some great photo-ops. That's the thing with Ladakh, almost everywhere you go, all you need is an instrument to click pictures and they will all be masterpieces. Honestly, unless you don't expect to visit Ladakh ever in your life (but really, how could you not be tempted to), don't go to an exhibition of Ladakh photos (or for that matter, the Himalaya in general) and buy them. So clear is the air, so large the scale, so sharp the colours, any photograph anyone takes is bound to be incredible.

## *Nubra valley*
We descended quickly and crossed the North Pullu

checkpoint. (Please don't form any romantic notions about South and North Pullu based on their cute names, they are just small army settlements, with no other purpose but to check who is passing through, or so we thought.)

The descent brings you down all the way to the river, and the sight invariably forces you out of the car in a bid to capture it, before you soon realize that's impossible and you just sit by the road and look at it. It's a wide river basin, couple of kilometres wide, dotted with squares of green cultivations, the aqua blue river snaking its way past them and small wooden bridges, appearing even smaller from the height of the road, connecting the banks to these cultivations. On both sides, you can see the river basin extending for miles, flanked by mountain ranges and the feeling of being small insignificant nothings, reappears. It's Ladakh, so the scale is obviously beyond imagination and visualization, but Nubra, according to me, is the ultimate mind-bender when it comes to sheer size of everything around you. A photograph is on page iii in the inserts.

A little further on we came across a big V formation, a mountain chain in the middle and riverbeds on both sides (Shyok meets Nubra river). The right side of the V goes on towards Siachen – civilians of course are not allowed all the way there. We took the left and soon were driving through the dried-up river bed itself towards Hunder, the place made famous by its sand dunes and Bactarian camels. Soon the sand dunes made their appearance, the smaller ones first eliciting a 'What's the big deal' from an impatient Arzoo, before the big deals started showing up. We turned right from the road onto the sand dunes and parked the car. The scene we saw pretty much encapsulates the growth in tourism Ladakh has seen over two-three years. When we came here in 2006, we had to first look for the camel herders, who then had to look for their camels in the bushes nearby. Almost an hour passed before they could track them down and fix seats on their backs. We were told to stay off them unless called and then noiselessly climb, and while taking a ride respect the animal.

Cut to 2010 and we were now in a parking lot with around forty cars and tourist buses. In front was a ticket counter with a long queue, the customary cold drink and snacks shop with leftovers thrown outside, another queue of people waiting their turn to ride the camels, and excited riders testing the patience of the emaciated camels. It was the classic catch-22 situation. You go to a nice place and want to tell the world about it, but then the world wants to go to that place and it can't stay nice anymore. Anyway, I am sure everyone who travels regularly faces such dilemmas, so I'll leave it at this. What affected me most was the plight of the camels. The proud Bactarian camels, with a double hump (and hence so nice to ride on) brought here a hundred years ago by some caravan on the Silk Route, have somehow managed to survive all these years. Their numbers haven't increased, there were still ten-twelve camels as in 2006, but their workload had. From letting visitors climb on their back once in a while, they are now employed full time in this business, without their consent of course, evident from their weak bodies and broken spirit. I shared my concerns with the group and we all decided not to ride. Instead, we walked for a while in the sand dunes with the snow-covered peaks in the background, took some photographs, threw some sand around, and returned.

## Packaged Ladakh

Ah, the lure of packaged trips. We will fly you into Leh, take you to Khardung La and Pangong, where 3 *Idiots* was shot, show you two monasteries and fly you back. Flight, stay, food and transportation, all-inclusive. But there is one thing they miss out on – Ladakh is very high. And with height come unpredictable weather and the necessity to acclimatize. One in three people who fly into Leh directly have a horrible time adjusting for the first two days at least, and by the time they do acclimatize, it's time for the flight back. Of course not everyone will admit to being pooped out on their great adventure and will instead focus on the photos at Pangong or the highest road in the world, etc. But that doesn't mean they didn't suffer. Now before this suffering becomes a 'it is like that only' kind of a phenomenon, know that there is a superb (and cheaper) alternative – drive from Kashmir to Leh, soak in Ladakh and arrive fully acclimatized. And by all means, fly out of Leh and save time there. Or else, drive back via Manali.

We stayed the night at a guesthouse in Hunder. 'Tomorrow we'll go to a hidden lake,' I announced, having decided to reveal my next card. Hidden lakes, flowering valleys, deadly gorges, phrases we all read in adventure stories and associate with fiction are very much real in the Himalaya and are guaranteed excitement boosters. 'It's a lake formed inside the mountain chain, in the middle of the river basin. Remember I showed you the V shape earlier? It's in the middle of the V. It's a fresh water lake and the locals consider it extremely sacred. I call it hidden because, when you're walking towards it, you can't see it till the very last moment.'

'Walking?'

Out of my entire monologue, Aliya had picked up just that one word.

'Yes, a bit of walking as the car can't go all the way. It's an easy walk,' I said reassuringly. She didn't seem convinced though.

The next morning we got up early and started driving towards Panamik village. Tourists used to visit this village largely to see the hot springs; these were later occupied by the army, who used them as a natural shower and washing machine. It's pretty dirty now and best avoided. We got out of the cars and climbed for about fifteen minutes, took a turn, sensed the lake before seeing it, quickened our pace and emerged right by its shore.

It's a small lake by Ladakh standards, with a circumference of less than a kilometre, but it's different. There are Buddhist prayer flags all around it, your voice echoes when you call out, the grassy shore tempts you into lying down and invariably people fall quiet and do just that.

It was soon time to head back to Leh. We were to leave

for a short two-day trek and homestay in Rumbak village the next day – the highlight of the trip, I had told everyone. So with music playing in the cars we settled in for the long drive to Leh over the Khardung La. 'Will reach Leh by 4 p.m. latest,' I said.

Ha.

## *We are not going anywhere today*

We reached the flat plateau just before the final climb to Khardung La by noon and immediately knew there was something wrong. More than fifty cars were parked there and there were signs of confusion everywhere. It didn't take long for us to hear the first rumour – there'd been another snowstorm the previous night; the road was blocked, but the army was clearing it. 'Okay, let's go to that dhaba there and eat something,' we decided. Some optimists decided to remain in the car and wait while the rest of us ordered a plate of momos at the dhaba.

As I looked around, I felt like we were in some sort of a global village: there were people from at least five-six countries there – Israelis, French, Americans, Australians and some other Indian tourists too – having tea or momos. Everyone seemed to be relaxed and not terribly bothered. As of now.

Half an hour passed and the next rumour flew in: the army had not been able to get their vehicles up from Leh, so it would take some more time. Well, too bad. 'Let's play cards,' someone said and we pulled out the lazy bums from the car, got our packs of cards out and started with badaam saat. Tea and pakoras were ordered. The couple running the dhaba were moving around purposefully;

they must have sensed it was time to bring on their A game.

'Excuse me, can you tell me what is happening,' a French girl, a single traveller, asked us, perhaps thinking we were the smart ones there who would know. We told her both the rumours we'd heard and added that we didn't know anything for sure. 'But there must be a way to find out,' she said. Hmmm, there must be, just that none of us had thought about it. 'Don't you think we all, as in Indians in general, are much more chilled out and patient, not that I'm saying this is a good or a bad thing,' remarked Kunal, eyeing the French girl with a patronizing look. 'But I can understand that she would be more concerned; it's not her country and she is travelling alone,' argued Pallavi. The rest of us kind of agreed with both of them.

Time flies when you are playing a game of cards, and when we next checked our watches it was well past 2 p.m. It was time for a loo break and also to find out what was latest in the rumour mills. 'Sir, there is an army control room over there. You please go and find out, they are not telling us anything,' was Tashi's suggestion. We walked towards the control room and joined a big throng outside. 'They are trying to get in touch with the top,' someone told us. As we jostled a bit further we heard, 'There is a chance it will not get cleared today', a little further and '4 p.m. is the deadline for today', and finally, 'There is a technical snag and we are trying to get the latest information', straight from the sharp-looking captain. He also confirmed that if they didn't get a clearance before 4 p.m., they would have to block the road for the night.

We had a quick group discussion and decided it was

best to return to Hunder and spend the night in the guesthouse. It seemed more and more unlikely that we would reach Leh tonight. And at 4.30 the message came: 'Come back early tomorrow morning.' As we drove back I told the group that if we managed to cross over early the next morning, there would still be time to go for our short trek to Rumbak village. The question was, what time would we be able to cross.

The next morning we started at 6 and by 7.30 we were at the checkpoint, our hopes of an immediate crossing dashed by the sight of a few other cars waiting in front. We followed yesterday's routine and were soon playing cards, sipping tea and eating momos at the dhaba. The couple running it had now been joined by two of their relatives in anticipation of a busy day.

Soon the dhaba started filling up and by 9 a.m. was bustling with activity. Then came the latest rumour – a truck was stranded on the road above and army vehicles were trying to clear it out of the way. A new twist. But the overall feeling still was that, come what may, we would be able to reach Leh today, pakka.

No one had been able to enter or leave Nubra valley for the last two days, so all faces were by now familiar, but there was a subtle difference in everyone's behaviour, especially the foreigners. They were now huddled closer together in two or three groups instead of sitting by themselves, like they had the previous day. They were obviously getting worried, as were many of us, but they were definitely more edgy. We felt it was a matter of time before something happened. Our game of cards was more interesting at the moment though, and we turned to it.

A game of cards is not just a game of cards; it's a stage where people sit together and chat, joke, pull each other's leg, order endless cups of tea and generally bond, especially when they don't know each other well. And in this case, it was also our way of insulating ourselves from what was turning out to be a big spanner in our plans.

'Why is it taking so long for one cup of tea,' we heard someone shout in a thick American accent. There you go. The simmering tension had come to the surface. There was a hustle in the kitchen and the lady hurried out with the tea. Arzoo and Upasana, who thought the two Americans were cute till yesterday, called them 'jerks'.

Looking at the situation objectively now, one can argue that if it were us stranded in a remote place in a remote part of an alien country, we would have been more worried than the locals as well. Perhaps, perhaps not. But the point is that at the time, we didn't feel their situation was any worse than ours. And we felt they had forced the words 'they' and 'us' through their behaviour.

It was almost noon by then and following is the sequence of events for the rest of the day: Rumour 4 – the truck is stuck at an angle that makes it impossible for it to be towed without it falling down the slope. Confirmed later by the army guys in a polite and calm manner. 'Don't worry sir, we are trying our best to get you all to Leh asap.'

A walk around the place. Discussions with other groups. Sharing of our plights – will miss my flight, my medicine is over, the foreigners are so fattu, etc. Back inside for more cards. News at 3 p.m. – chances are the road will not open today either. Mass depression. Meeting with my group –

we will not drive all the way back to Hunder; let's stay in the village below. News at 4 p.m. – road won't open today.

There wasn't much we could do so we decided to accept the situation and try something different today. Khardung village was just thirty minutes from there. We stopped our cars on the road and Aliya, Tashi and I went and knocked on the door of the biggest home in the village. An old man opened the door and we told him our situation and requested him to let us stay in his house. Tashi also pitched in and Aliya smiled innocently. Perfect. He agreed in so little time, I almost got the feeling he was hoping someone would come and stay in his house!

We whistled to the rest of the group and waved them in. It was a biggish house with three rooms including a living room. We moved the furniture from the living room and put gaddas on the carpet for all of us to sleep. Tashi and Sonam helped the family (the man's wife and a young son) cook a simple but delicious meal and for the entire evening we didn't think about the fact that we were well and truly stranded in Nubra valley.

Later, under a full moon, with the snow shining on the peaks around us, I told the group about the 'chakwa' concept (in Maharashtra, a chakwa is a mischievous ghost who plays a prank on you so that you keep coming back to the same place you started from), and told them that now we have broken the jinx by staying at a different place, we would surely get out tomorrow. This amused everyone. More ghost stories followed and the host family also joined in, curious about why we were making so much of a fuss. Later they brought in a lot of blankets, it was bitterly cold don't forget, and the combined warmth of pure yak wool blankets and the eight of us together in one room ensured we had a good sleep.

Tashi, in his optimist avatar now, woke us at 6 a.m., and by 7 a.m., after a breakfast of Ladakhi bread and butter tea, we were off to the all too familiar dhaba. I must mention that the holding area itself was very pretty – a photograph is on page iv in the inserts; but since we were forced to stay there we weren't able to appreciate its beauty that much.

## *The D-day*

By virtue of staying the night in Khardung village, we were amongst the first ones to reach the dhaba and grabbed the best seats. It didn't surprise us anymore that the road was still not open, no work can happen at night on the road, and we knew it would be some time before news/rumours started coming in.

Another round of breakfast, rueful smiles exchanged with the usual suspects trickling in, cards brought out, and so began another typical day in Nubra valley. Everyone was watching out for the foreigners to see their reaction at having to wait again. But today, they came with a strategy. And the strategy was to pressurize the army guys non-stop. Every ten minutes a few of them would walk to the Army control room, where we could see them gesturing wildly, and then return with their voices louder, more confused, one step closer to completely losing it.

'They are threatening the army guys and demanding a helicopter rescue,' someone informed us. Wow. We followed the next contingent to the control room and figured that there were just a couple of them who were ultra-aggressive; the rest were trying to be rational, but getting dragged along by the more belligerent ones. 'Sir, we can't get a helicopter just for your group. Most likely the road will open today, if not, the army has already planned for a helicopter rescue of everyone stranded here by tomorrow. You must understand it is very, very high and the helicopters struggle at this altitude. It's not so straightforward.' The captain must have said the same thing countless times in the same calm tone.

It was disappointing to find out that there was a chance that we wouldn't get out even today, but it was also clear that it was not for a lack of effort from the army. The conditions were just too difficult. Come to think of it, just the fact that there is a fully functional road there is a miracle in itself. Because of the altitude and the narrow road, big recovery vehicles can't climb up and the lighter ones were having a tough time getting the truck cleared. On top of that, there was intermittent snowfall daily and temperatures would drop to below freezing.

As we were roaming outside the dhaba, doing time pass, we heard loud shouting from inside. It had happened. We rushed in to see a bunch of Indians arguing loudly with some of the foreigners. Apparently, they had been loudly cursing the army and India in general, and a group sitting close by had had enough of it. On one side were a bunch of three, a boy and two girls from Chennai. On the other were the two Americans, the French girl and a couple. 'The army is not doing anything.' 'How do you know?' 'It can't take two days to clear a road.' 'But it is not an ordinary road.' 'Bullshit.' 'Bullshit what?' 'Bullshit this place, this army, this country.' 'Who asked you to come here then? You guys come because you want to travel cheap.'

I could see everyone was particularly angry about the comments against the army.

'For all you know, no one is even trying to clear the truck. It's my last time in India for sure, if I ever get out of this place.' 'Don't worry, no one has an agenda to keep you guys here. Not that you contribute much to the local economy. You are always haggling over room and food cost.'

Oh boy! Little off the topic, but it wasn't the most sensible argument to begin with.

'The army has been lying to us for two days.' 'Why would they lie, you can clearly make out they are constantly working. You guys have not done your research or what before coming to Ladakh? It is not Goa. It's a tough place and these kind of things can and do happen here. All of us are in the same situation, but we are not panicking.' The Chennai girls were on fire.

Perhaps the foreigners didn't expect all of us to gang up on them like this, and decided to retreat and keep their feelings to themselves.

'How can they say anything against our army?' Upasana was furious. And the overall mood was not different from this. Altitude-induced, foreigner-triggered patriotism at 4500m. Maybe not; maybe it's just that the army is one entity that brings out the feeling of nationalism in all of us; the altitude just made us very vocal about it. The altitude and the blatantly unfair accusations. Tension simmered inside the dhaba for the rest of the afternoon.

Meanwhile we also started getting hourly updates about the road situation. At 2 p.m., the news came that the truck has finally been straightened and was now getting towed to a safe and broad part of the road. Not an easy task once again. Tashi came to us and told us to remain together and be ready to run to the car as there would be a major rush towards the road. The seriousness with which he said this would have made us laugh if not for our own state of mind. Instead, we pulled our stuff closer to us, tied our shoelaces (just kidding), and were all set.

## *The final rush*

Minutes ticked by. Everyone on high alert. People thinking twice even before going to pee. Drivers shuttling back and forth between the dhaba and the control room. Checking their tyres. Turning steering wheels toward the road. Tense stuff. Couple of false alarms with people rushing out from the dhaba only to be sent back in. It was unbelievable. Our only aim in life was to cross over to Leh.

And then, 'Khul gaya, jaldi aao'. The mad race started. People pretended to be in a movie as they jumped over tables to get out of the dhaba and ran like crazy to their respective cars. Then ran back to collect the bag that had slipped from their back. Cars honking. People getting into wrong cars – they all looked similar. Cars driving off while people were still getting in. Drivers screaming at the cars in front that were blocking them because their passengers had not yet come. Dust flying everywhere. No Hollywood or Indian movie could have captured that craziness.

And then, the calm. Everyone overwhelmed. Cars moving along in a single file, and not much to be done now except hope they keep moving. (A photograph clicked in the dark on page iv in the inserts.) An army jeep was in front of the caravan of about fifty cars, setting the pace. We reached North Pullu at about 5:30 p.m. and saw a bunch of exhausted-looking soldiers, the ones who had spent the last three days clearing the road, with their JCBs and the recovery cranes. They were sitting by the side of the road, having a cup of tea, smiling and waving to us. I am sure all of us felt good about taking their side in the argument earlier in the day.

As we crawled on, we faced a new problem. It was getting dark and we were still an hour away from the top – and the descent into Leh yet to be made. As the sun goes down, frost appears on the road and it becomes very slippery: every Himalayan driver's nightmare. Again, we'd underestimated the army. At every tricky spot on the route, there were a bunch of soldiers positioned to help the vehicles pass by. They had powerful lights and tools to guide each vehicle around the corner. They then messaged the next station that so many vehicles have crossed and are approaching them. It was super stuff.

As we looked back we could see the lights of the caravan stretching for over 2 km. Soon we passed the old, harmless-looking truck, the culprit if we could call it that. The over-enthu driver had tried to cross the pass late in the evening, skidded and was lucky to survive.

By the time we reached the top of Khardung La, it was almost 8 p.m. – the regular closing time is 6 p.m. At the top there wasn't the usual enthusiasm to take photos or buy souvenirs; in fact we barely stopped for a breather before we pressed on. The descent turned out to be much easier since the road was in better condition here. Tashi relaxed as well and began playing his Himesh Reshamiya CD. And we could finally appreciate the haunting beauty of the snow-covered mountains under a full moon, the tough, unforgiving terrain through which the road passed, the lights of Leh in the distance twinkling like the stars above us, the absolute stillness and majesty of Ladakh.

\* \* \*

## *Raju, the Guide*
*Short mein bole toh, Ladakh is not your regular hill station, go there well prepared.*

### More reading
Some easily available books and guides that I have managed to read and gained from (there are many books on Ladakh; these are just the ones I have on my bookshelf right now):

| Title | Category | Author | Remarks |
|---|---|---|---|
| *A Journey in Ladakh* (1983) | Travel and spirituality | Andrew Harvey | Account of the author's travels in Ladakh, with an open mind and a keen eye. |
| *Trekking in Ladakh* – a Trailblazer guide (Updated in 2004) | Guidebook | Charlie Loram | Easily the best guide to trekking anywhere in Ladakh, especially because of the detailed maps. |

| Ladakh Adventure and *The Snow Leopard Adventure* (2013) | Adventure fiction for young adults | Deepak Dalal | Thoroughly enjoyable way to find out about Ladakh. |

## What else to do in Ladakh

*Trekking* – It's currently one of the most popular trekking destinations in the Indian Himalaya, and rightly so. It is vast, it has innumerable trekking routes of all difficulty levels, there are very good local trekking agencies you can hire and weather is more predictable than in other parts of the Himalaya. Just don't do the typical thing of going on the same two to three treks that most of the trekkers go on (Markha valley and Padum-Darcha). Spread out, there are so many options, just ask.

*Car/bike riders* – Well, Ladakh is at the top in this segment too. People buy bikes later, and dream of going to Ladakh first. It's okay, I guess, as long as it's done with the spirit of adventure and not wannabe machismo. Too many bikers crying and kicking their bikes have been spotted on the roads.

*Chilling out* – If you are looking for a quiet time in Leh, skip July and August and you will be well rewarded. Leh has managed to retain its coolness factor and some really hep cafés, eating places, etc. dot the market, the best ones just off the main streets.

*Winter sports* – Ah, the next big thing perhaps. Polo, ice skating and monastery festivals can make the bitterest winter fun.

## Point to be noted

What's up with this fascination of driving to Ladakh from the Manali side? Hello, if it's fear that's keeping you from Kashmir, you are a decade behind in time. But my guess is that you just don't know better. Because everyone is going from Manali, so will you. Okay, there are two things here: a) The road from Srinagar to Leh via Kargil climbs at a much steadier rate, crucial for acclimatization and b) It is as stunning, wild, etc., etc., if not more than the Manali-Leh one. The way to Ladakh has always been through Kashmir. You can return via Manali, if you like. This will make sure you don't suffer on the 5000m passes on that road and can actually enjoy them.

## Local service providers

Snow Leopard Conservancy runs a wide network of homestays in some of the most beautiful and accessible Ladakhi villages. You shouldn't come back from Ladakh without staying in one. http://www.himalayan-homestays.com.

If you plan to trek or book homestays in Ladakh, I would recommend the Ladakh Women Travel Company, LWTC, a one of its kind all-women adventure travel agency. http://www.ladakhiwomenstravel.com.

For guesthouses in Leh, there are still a few left in Changspa area that are authentic family-run establishments, something Leh was famous for. Try Jigmet guesthouse, or just drop by and check out the many other small ones.

Story 3

# The High of Kulu Valley

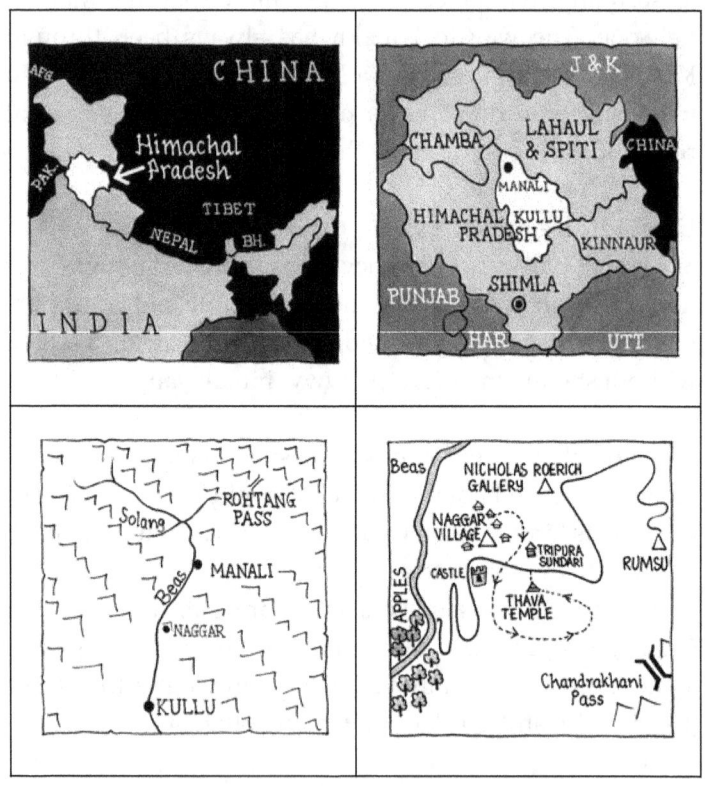

Hand-drawn maps for representation purpose only. Not to scale.

## *The setting*

As you cross over the Rohtang Pass while returning from Ladakh to Manali, something dramatic happens. Well, everything in Himalaya is dramatic you could argue, but we are talking of top drawer dramatic here. As the road morphs into a path through slush and broken stones, you won't be able to take your eyes off the stupendously green valley looming in front. Not the proper Kulu valley as yet, but the precursor to it. On both sides are green mountains, still very high mind you, and in the middle are small streams creating space for themselves, slowly but steadily. Come down further and you can see the valley opening up as if the mountains on both sides have been parted by the hands of God, the streams all joining to form a river, and the first signs of habitation. Soon the Solang stream also joins the river and the Beas roars ahead. Now if you look up, you will realize the uniqueness of this valley – it's locked in by high mountains on three sides. If you were a king in times past you would look at it this way: abundant water, abundant cultivable land, natural protection from three sides. A big smile.

The Kulu valley stretches from the base of Rohtang Pass, through Manali, Kulu town and then to Mandi, further downstream. At some places the valley is a couple of kilometres wide, and these days most of this stretch is covered with apple orchards, the game changer in the Kulu economy. Not that other fruits are not cultivated, they very much are, but the apples dominate.

## *The stage*

Now, as the king of this valley, you would want to keep a

watch over the entire stretch, or as much of it as possible, so obviously your capital has to be a place somewhat higher up in the mountains, and not in the valley. Which is why Naggar came into being, and stayed as the valley's capital city for centuries, and till very recently, before Manali became a tourist hub, it was the centre of the Kulu valley.

As a king, you would also build a castle for yourself, and you will build it in a way that it blends with the surroundings, use readily available wood and stone, and build it at the spot with the best view of the valley. The 16th century castle in Naggar stands till date, and since its renovation by HPTDC, is actually a very good place to stay and survey the valley below as kings would have done for ages.

We fell in love with Naggar when we first went there. It's quiet and calm, so different from the hustle-bustle of Manali (we weren't looking for hustle-bustle you see, we get enough of that in Mumbai), and the way it does justice to that oft-abused word – charming.

## *The cast*
The kids playing basketball in Naggar square, the sadhu at the hidden shrine, the resident family in Thava, the Russian tourists and our group of eight.

## *The act: A path less travelled and the lost city of Thava*
'New year in the Himalaya? In that cold? We're on.'

And so, with Rajiv and Sarika on board, we were eight of us for the 'New Year's High' trip. It was 2008. New Year's Eve in Mumbai was getting monotonous; you were more likely to bring in the new year stuck in an endless traffic jam than in the truly fun, cool or crazy manner people aim for. So what better than to head towards the good old mountains, with the guaranteed space, peace, quiet and a certain level of craziness too.

'Just make friends with the cold,' was my only instruction, which was misinterpreted by most on the group as a green signal to pack in woollens, jackets, mufflers, leg warmers, and what not. And so with suitcases the size of almirahs, we reached Naggar castle late one night in the last week of December.

Cut to next morning, a big breakfast table set up in the courtyard of the castle in bright sunshine, with a leafless tree in the middle, snow-covered range in front and the Kulu valley awash in winter colours stretched as far as one could see. Maybe a photo will help here; see the one on page v in the inserts. Trust me, a moment in the warmth of the winter sun is worth freezing your ass for hours. I don't know how else to put it; it just makes you happy. And so, over hot paranthas, butter, omelettes and chai, a happy bunch discussed plans for the rest of the day.

'Let's start from the village and the temple of Gauri Shankar, then on to the beautiful temple of Tripura Sundari in the heart of Naggar, from there we'll follow a trail through the forest to a hidden shrine and finally to the Krishna temple of Thava, about which I don't know much. This should take us three hours max and we can then come back for lunch,' I summarized.

There are roughly two kinds of temple architecture in the Kulu valley (and to a certain extent in the western Himalaya, barring the trans-Himalaya): the shila style and the pagoda style. The Gauri Shankar temple is a shila style temple, that is, it's made of blocks of stone piled on top of each other and starting from a rectangular base it merges in a conical shape at the top. The temple has a courtyard laid out with the same blocks of stone in front and, as always, a lovely view.

The clear blue sky promised a long day of sunshine and we took our time ambling along the lanes of Naggar, passing the two-storey wooden homes where inhabitants idled on their porch, enjoying the sun and smiling at us. Some of these houses are a couple of hundred years old, and apart from being lovely to look at, are well insulated due to the exclusive use of wood and stone (not to mention earthquake proof because of the tiny gaps between stones or logs of wood). It's such a pity that, everywhere in the Himalaya, the display of wealth means resorting to a brick and mortar home, like they see in the plains.

A little ahead we came across a bunch of kids playing, of all things, basketball. I have seen volleyball being played with gusto in almost every Himalayan village, but this was a first. We shot a couple, missed, were laughed at and given a demo of how it's done. These kids were barely ten years old. Naggar basketball association, we named it, feeling very smart, and continued ahead.

Mid-way between Naggar castle and the Nicholas Roerich gallery is the centre-piece of Naggar, the Tripura Sundari temple. Overzealous government officials and wealthy locals have conspired to 'modernize' this temple and have built an ugly construction right in front, but thankfully the original structure survives, and viewed from the side, still presents a very pretty sight. It's a pagoda-style temple, with three diminishing layers of the wooden roof rising above each other. Dedicated to the Goddess, the oldest and best sculptures are foolishly kept outside, and a new statue of Durga takes their place in the sanctum sanctorum. The engravings in stone and wood are unique, depicting the tantric origins of the temple. 'Lucky we got to see all this before they decided to get rid of it altogether!' I commented.

## *Standardizing the gods*

A little rant is due about the mindless conversion of unique temples, especially in the Himalaya, dedicated to native devis, devtas, rocks, trees and other forms of nature, into mainstream Hinduism. The most pronounced standardization is in statues of native goddesses. No matter how fascinating her history and story specific to that region, it's promptly replaced by a marble Durga, the same deity that you will see in almost every temple in north India. This is usually carried out by overzealous politicians or rich villagers to show off their 'contribution' or to imply that

> now this temple has joined the big league. I mean, there won't be a school for miles, but all temples must have marble statues. Very soon, the only surviving records of the famous Himalayan temples (forget about the less popular and smaller ones) will be in books written by a few enthusiastic scholars.

I was told to chill and a quick diversion to the German Bakery was proposed. Good idea. Not that we were tired or anything, but the coffee and cake were too tempting. It's the relaxed nature of a Himalayan holiday I guess, that makes you savour the smallest things. We then returned past the castle and left the road to follow a narrow trail climbing up and into the forest. Within minutes it was as if we were in a different world altogether. It's amazing how just a few metres of forest insulates you from the road, the noise, everything, and sucks you into a place where there is just you, the trail, the trees and bushes all around. And the only sounds are of you breathing, that of birds and sometimes of flowing water, which can be heard for miles. We were excited now; wilderness is infectious, you see.

After about fifteen or twenty minutes, we came across a stream. On the opposite bank, which can be reached by a narrow log bridge, was the shrine of a rishi. The setting couldn't have been better for the rishi to be away from the world, but still close enough, and meditate and do all those things that rishis do. We crossed over and climbed up to the temple, to find it locked. 'Not that they were expecting us or anything,' Zahir stated wisely. But after a quick search around the temple, we located the caretaker sadhu, who got really excited on seeing us, they love occasional company, all these dwellers in the uninhabited, and he literally ran down from his room to open the padlock. A quick peek inside was followed by a long gossip session with him, wherein he enlightened us on topics ranging from religion to politics to wildlife, everything. 'Idhar sher aata hai?' asked Sarika, keeping alive the tradition of at least one person in the group on every single trip asking this question, and giving the 'expert' an opportunity to indulge himself. 'Bahut bada bagh aaya tha kuch din pehle, hum nahi darte.'

We asked for directions to the temple at Thava and continued onwards. The trail now climbed above the forest and passed through open expanses of land, some cultivated and some pastures. In the middle of each of these fields were small log huts, most of them in various states of disuse. These were most likely the infamous dwellings of the 'hippies' and other such assorted crowd that descended into the Kulu and Parvati valleys during the 'golden age of weed tourism', decided it was too cumbersome to keep going back and forth between countries, and chose to stay here instead, permanently, and illegally.

The locals were first amused, it was just weed after all, they don't even bother with this grass, but embraced the super profitable 'tourism' very soon. Trails start from here and go on to cross the mind-blowingly beautiful Chandrakhani Pass and then to the village, or should I say, the democratic republic of Malana, the birthplace of THE malana cream (the biggest brand name in the world of marijuana). Even now, if you trek here, in Parvati valley especially, you will come across some very brave foreigner, living on either side of the thin line between tourists and felons, but doing so on a high.

Unknowingly trampling some weed plants under our feet (it pretty much grows wild everywhere), we walked towards a couple in one of the terraced fields to ask them for directions to Thava temple. 'Yeh jungle ke raste se jaao, short cut,' the woman replied, with a smile so pretty, Mahesh said he would have 'taken the short cut to hell if she'd asked'. Not sure if there has been a study done on the effects of inhaling air around where weed is grown, but MJ would have been a good subject that day!

The 'jungle ka rasta' turned out to be bit more wild than we expected, broken at parts, but it was definitely short, and in less than ten minutes we could see a temple ahead. A shila-style temple, which was a surprise considering its distance from Naggar and it being almost in the middle of a jungle. As we approached it, we could see a compound in front and an old man standing outside.

He must have been surprised to see a bunch of us, obviously not natives, emerging from the thick bushes, but was composed enough to say namaste and pointed us in through the wooden door of the compound. We entered a porch, where we took off our shoes, and in front was a big rectangular courtyard. Straight ahead was a huge tulsi plant and in front of it was the main temple. On our right were two small rooms, for the old man's family we guessed, and the left was unenclosed, facing the wide open Kulu valley and affording a view if not better, at par with the Naggar castle.

All of us instinctively went for the view and sat on the parapet looking at it, admiring it, resting our legs, clicking photos, and for a change, not talking too much. Picture time – it's on page v in the inserts.

## *Reality check*

**Zahir Mirza**
**The ad guy, Doosra Consultancy Pvt Ltd**

*The memory of Naggar is as fresh as if it happened yesterday.*

*A bunch of city slickers shepherded by GP and regimented by Rujuta. Rajiv walked with his Blackberry Bold, Manu with his memories, Sarika with Rajiv and his Blackberry, Bhavana with her opinions, Mahesh with his knowledge, Madhav with his conscience, and I with cynicism. We looked anything but adventure seekers.*

*We walked up the hill, Rajiv and Sarika trailing behind, Madhav and GP leading the way, with no idea of what to expect. And then we saw how the hill sparkled so much in the sunshine, it looked golden. The gang, usually busy chatting, became still. There was something about the hill and the temples we visited that morning.*

*This one walk on the hill changed the whole group. Rajiv and Sarika were walking – no, bouncing – like little children. Madhav, Manu and GP were a group, as if catching up on all their wrongdoings in the college they had studied in together.*

*Mahesh was rolling with laughter, and Bhavana was amused. I was still – walking, huffing and puffing – but still. This was soon after my divorce and I found all the answers I wanted. We found stones amusing and a reed meaningful. It was clear that nature had reclaimed each one of us.*

*We walked back to the hotel feeling much lighter that late afternoon.*

\* \* \*

'Where are you from?' asked a young woman in halting but decent English. She was the daughter-in-law of the caretaker panditji of the temple, the old man we had met outside, she told us. 'And how come you know English?' I asked rather stupidly. 'I went to school and college,' came the matter-of-fact reply. 'Panditji is waiting for you inside the temple, go and see.'

As we entered the main temple structure, we were surprised by the vast amount of space inside. Even to untrained eyes like ours, we could make out that this portion of the temple was added much later as compared to the sanctum sanctorum, which looked positively ancient with its old rock walls. Inside was an idol of Krishna and Gauri, which was relatively new again, but unlike in so many temples I have seen, the original, a jet black rock cut statue of Krishna was prominently displayed and the panditji looked fondly at it and told us it was more than 1,500 years old!

Wait a minute: 1,500 years? That's really, really old. 'Pandra sau saal?' Rajiv asked, with a hint of disbelief that was mirrored on most of our faces. 'It has to be a historic site then. How come it's not so popular?' 'It *is* a historic site, the oldest in Kulu. Haven't you heard about the lost city of Thava?' Panditji spoke in Hindi.

Ooh, a lost city and all, who knew we would stumble upon one on our ramble. Panditji continued. 'Thava was the biggest city in Kulu valley at one point and was also the original capital. Our elders told us that after the Mahabharata war, the Pandavas came here and built a castle on the hills – its ruins can still be seen. But then, in the 6th century, it was totally destroyed by a big earthquake, everything except this temple, which was damaged, but miraculously survived.' He was dead serious.

Earthquakes destroying entire towns in the Himalaya is not unheard of, it has happened in the recent past with Uttarkashi, so that was plausible, but it was still surprising that such an old temple existed, along with a very interesting story so close to Naggar and Manali and that no one talks about it. Panditji asked us to go around the temple once and as we did so, looking at it from a different perspective. We saw the tilt in the structure – it leaned towards the left (photo on page v in the inserts) – the unique carvings on its walls (at least they looked very different to us), the rath standing at the back (a common sight in important Himalayan temples as the devtas are taken out on some occasions on these chariots) and the strategic view of the Kulu valley. None of these factors proved that the temple was a historic one, but then, neither did they disprove it.

## *Jab we wed*

In 2011, Rujuta and I were in Kulu valley during the monsoon; it's almost an annual ritual with us. We visited the temple at Thava and fell in love with it all over again. Enough to ask Jaydevji, the panditji there, 'Do people get married here? It seems like a great place to get married.' 'Of course. People get married here all the time.' 'You can get us married?' Out of the blue. 'Ah, yes,' he said, looking tentatively at us. 'Your parents know about this?' 'No, we just decided one minute ago, but of course we will call our respective families. When can you get us married?' He consulted his almanac and declared Sunday to be a great day. It was Thursday then. 'And how much will it cost?' He did some mental calculations, counted on his fingers, and declared, 'Rs 5000 for the ceremony and food afterwards for fifteen people.' We must have looked like we'd just won a lottery.

We walked down to a coffee shop, where we washed down what had just happened with a cup of coffee. Then frantic calls were made to parents, siblings, close friends, and they must love us

> dearly as they all assembled in Naggar by Saturday night. Our local drivers, who were also invited as representatives of Naggar, got us a Kulu cap and shawl each. The ceremony in the temple was short and meaningful. Panditji married us in the pahari style, explaining the rituals, and in twenty minutes it was over. We then sat outside in the veranda and were served local dishes. It was unbelievably yummy and most of our family and friends seem to remember the meal more than the fact that we got married.

Jaydevji, that was the name of the panditji, asked us to have a cup of tea before leaving, and as we waited out in the courtyard, a group of four girls, all foreigners, came in, took off their shoes, picked up brooms and a water bucket, and started cleaning the compound. Before it got any weirder, the daughter-in-law, with her three-month-old daughter Priyasakhi tied on her back, came to us with tea and explained. The place is apparently very popular with Russian tourists, especially women, who come here through the year, stay in a small guesthouse behind the temple, are provided with food by Panditji's family and in return do various chores around the temple. All this happens with little or no communication between the two parties because of the language barrier. You are free to speculate about their motives for staying here based on the facts presented earlier. Thava really was just full of surprises.

As we walked down from the temple to Naggar, ran down rather, we all had the expression of those who got much more than they had set out for. The shortcut (again) deposited us in the middle of Naggar in about ten minutes and in just the right mood for a nice hot lunch in the balcony of the castle. Which in turn, as it overlooks the winter sun-washed valley, puts one in a contemplative mood. And, I can speak for all of us there, we did do some contemplation: the 'simplicity' of our walk today, how without ever feeling like explorers we'd explored, without wanting anything out of the act, we were rewarded, the four temples, the stream, the forest, the log huts, the lost city of Thava, things that sound so enchanting and otherworldly when spoken about, didn't seem to be a step out of the ordinary when we were there, part of the scene. But then again, as we ate rice with rajma and siddu (Himachali curd), sitting in the balcony of a 16th century castle made of only wood and stone, in line with the snow on the mountain chain opposite us, and a thousand feet above the Beas river flowing down through apple orchards, it could have occurred to us that when in Himalaya, extraordinary is the norm.

* * *

## *Raju, the Guide*
*Short mein bole toh, Naggar is the definitive place to go to in the Kulu valley.*

### More reading
Some easily-available books and guides that I have managed to read and gain from (books mentioned are about Himachal in general, which also cover Naggar):

| Title | Category | Author | Remarks |
|---|---|---|---|
| *The Temples of Himachal* | Special interest | Govt of Himachal | Gives a good account of temples all over Himachal. |

| *Himachal Pradesh* (1993) | History and people | Hari Krishan Mittoo | A concise account of the history, places and people. |
| --- | --- | --- | --- |
| *Guide to Trekking in Himachal* (2003) | Guidebook | Minakshi Chaudhry | She describes 63 treks that she did, with maps, distances, etc. A very handy book. |

## What to do in Kulu valley

*Trekking* – This goes without saying, Manali being the adventure hub and all. But sadly, the only trek the trekking agencies are interested in is the one to Beas kund, or in that direction. On a typical summer day, you will meet hundreds, if not more, people huffing and puffing their way up and down, feeling God knows what about walking on trails littered with plastic wrappers and discarded bottles. There are semi-permanent camps set up on the route where hundreds of students from all over India, in a failed attempt by school authorities and parents to give the kids an 'outdoor' holiday, are hoarded together like sheep and made to do some inane 'activities'.

Okay, enough with the cribbing. There are some fantastic trekking opportunities in Kulu and the surrounding valleys:

— There are passes that you can cross to reach Lahaul, on the other side of Rohtang.
— Or you can explore the right bank of the Beas, further down towards Katrain. You can walk to the small

villages high on the hills or go for the Bara Banghal trek, the ultimate adventure in Kulu valley.
— And of course the trek over Chandarkhani Pass to Parvati valley and multiple treks in Parvati valley thereon.
— Coming up next on the adventure map of the region is the Greater Himalayan National Park in nearby Sainj valley with its multiple trekking, camping and bird-watching opportunities. Gushaini is a quaint village and entry point to GHNP. Raju's Cottage is *the* place to stay in Gushaini.

*Rafting* – There are plenty of rafting agencies all along the Beas. But pick the stretch that is to your liking and ask about the difficulty level.

*Chilling out* – That's what I do most of the time when in Kulu valley. Naggar is, of course, a superb base for chilling anytime in the year, but if you can brave the monsoon – the uncertainty of roads getting washed away and all that – the entire valley is at its best then, mist over the Beas and apples hanging from trees.

**Point to be noted**

Naggar is just 20 km from Manali, and if you have seen what has happened to Manali it shouldn't be a tough choice to choose to stay here instead. Only recently have 'day tourists' started flocking to see the castle and the Nicholas Roerich art gallery (a must-see by the way), but more to tick them off the list. Visit the temple in Thava or go anywhere above the Naggar town on countless trails leading to some beautiful vistas in less than fifteen minutes of walking. Highly recommended is the short climb to the village of **Rumsu**, and for a day trip a drive to the hidden, mystical, beautiful, **Parashar lake** above Kulu.

### Special note
Here comes my Bollywood connection. Ayan Mukherji, who directed *Yeh Jawaani, Hai Deewani* is an avid trekker himself and I helped him with locations in Kulu to shoot the trekking scenes, etc. in the film. These are the places in and around Kulu valley where the movie was shot (and trust me they look as good in reality as they did on the screen) – Katrain village on the Beas, Jalori pass (camping site) in the Parvati valley and the deodar forest near Marhi on the way to Rohtang Pass.

### Local service providers
You won't need any if you are planning to chill anywhere in Kulu valley. Just hire a local cab and drive around. For trekking around Naggar, I prefer smaller agencies in the town as compared to the ones in Manali. Speak with a few of them and make a decision. For the Bara Banghal trek, you could consider www.bharmourtreks.com.

# Story 4

# Surreal Spiti

Hand-drawn maps for representation purpose only. Not to scale.

## *The setting*

Beyond the greater Himalayan ranges lies the trans-Himalaya, also known as the cold desert or Tibetan plateau. That plateau – actually it's not a plateau in the true sense of the word; there are mountain chains, rivers and valleys too – extends from Ladakh through Zanskar, then Spiti and proper Tibet itself. Its unimaginable scale, crystal-sharp colours (mainly shades of brown) and its essential nature as a wild, untamed land is a magnet that attracts and doesn't let go.

In Himachal, the greater Himalayan ranges pass through Kulu and Kinnaur, separating them from Lahaul and Spiti which become the trans-Himalayan regions. Spiti in particular is unique. It's actually a collection of small villages along the Spiti river (and some of its tributaries), most of which are situated not on the banks but high up in the mountains. That's where the pastures are which are crucial for their cattle to graze on. The name Spiti has been interpreted as the 'middle land' also; the middle land between Indian Himalayan regions and Tibet or middle land between heaven and Earth, I'm not sure.

As landlocked goes, Spiti is a perfect example, just that the locks are some of the highest mountains in the world. Completely impenetrable except over some extremely high passes, Spiti remained more or less unaffected by the political and territorial upheavals that its neighbours Ladakh and Kinnaur faced. This kept it from 'developing', in the sense that there was no contact with the outside world, no exchange of ideas, and so on, but what this did was allow it to retain its culture and religion (Tibetan Buddhism) in the purest form. What Spiti is today (religiously speaking) is what Tibet at its peak must have been like. And believe it or not, centuries of isolation have given Spiti a quality that cannot be described, only experienced.

### The young lama

'For how long will you stay in the monastery?' 'Marne tak.' We were silent for a few minutes after the twelve-year-old Dorje Phonchuk said this with a smile and a matter-of-fact tone (maybe there was an uncomfortable giggle in between). In Spiti, the first son inherits the land, the second becomes a monk and the third is educated. A tradition dictated more by the economics of the land (limited cultivable land) than any other factor.

We were in Dorje's family homestay in Demul (a village at 4300m). Homestays are a concept started not too long ago by Snow Leopard Conservancy in Ladakh. This way, visitors, instead of pitching tents in village farmland (which benefits nobody), enjoy the warm Spitian hospitality and the host family gains financially. Probably the best of all sustainable tourism initiatives.

The child lama had a calmness belying his age. 'Do you miss home?' 'Yes.' 'What do you do then?' 'I play really hard that evening.' Sorted, this guy was. He lives in Komic monastery, amongst the highest in the world at 4300m, and belonging to the Sakyapa sect of Tibetan Buddhism. What this means is that, unlike the older sect (Nyingmapa), he will not lead a family life and will be celibate for the rest of his life. He goes to a regular school in the morning and has his classes for Buddhist teachings in the afternoon before he gets to his evening round of volleyball and running around. His regular schooling will end once he finishes 5th grade, and from then on it's a hardcore monastic life for him. And he is ready for that.

He was home on a rare vacation. A time he spent with his entire family reaping the crop of peas, the sweet-tasting matars that the whole of Spiti was harvesting at the moment.

'Shouldn't we do something about Dorje being sent to the monastery?' A lot of us asked this question or at least thought about it. I guess what we need to understand is that this system has been going on for ages and is therefore something that has worked. A mixture of pragmatism and belief, it's the way of life for them which of course we will not be able to comprehend. Dorje Phonchuk is a happy lama. He will be fine.

Across the mountains southwest of Spiti is Kinnaur, the land of half god-half men, the mythical Kinnaras or the celestial musicians as per the scriptures. The culture here is a unique mix of Hinduism, nature-worship and Tibetan Buddhism. There are some unique festivals here that deserve a story of their own, but I'll leave it for another time. The overwhelming quality of Kinnaur though is its greenery, from the 'it's so pretty it's unreal' Sangla valley to the mountain villages of Kalpa and Sarahan, it's the hundreds of shades of green flanked by the snow-covered peaks and the blue skies which must have given it its mythical status. From the point of view of our story just note that it's as different from Spiti as possible.

## *The stage*
To travel from Kinnaur to Spiti, the shortest route till very recently was to cross over the Srikhand Mahadev range using any of the four or five accessible passes. Now there is a road that goes around the mountains, but trust me, you don't want to miss what's in store for you on any of these trails. Ask the locals, who still prefer walking over the passes than taking the road.

Amongst the most accessible and prettiest trails is the one leading from Bhabha valley in Kinnaur to Pin valley in Spiti over the Wang khango (khango means pass in the local dialect), or more commonly used name, the Pin-Bhabha Pass. Now, I haven't been on any of the other trails from Kinnaur to Spiti, but I can't imagine anything being prettier than the Pin-Bhabha trail. Of course I am bound to be proved wrong, but let me be. It's a four-day trek for mortals and a two, or max three-day one, for locals. And over each of these four days, the scenery changes so dramatically that for a long time after the trek is over you will catch yourself catching up with all that you have seen.

## *The cast*
Gatuk, our guide, Lobzang, the cook, Tshering, the donkey man, four donkeys, the veterinarian of Kara, Rujuta and I. And a man, no a person, no a thing ... well, just read on.

## *The act: The pastures of Kara and the friendly spirit phenomenon*
'Wait ... I am dying ... you are walking too fast ... what nonsense.' It took me more than two minutes to say this sentence between long gasps for air.

We had just begun the climb through the forest above Kafnu on the first day of the trek and I was complaining bitterly to Rujuta for not paying heed to her partner's struggles. I was jealous of course, but I pretended to pity her for her inability to 'feel' what one is supposed to on a climb like this.

The oak and fir forest was thick and therefore dark, and the zigzag trail climbed relentlessly through it. That we had been walking happily along the same trail just ten minutes back as it meandered along the Bhabha stream seemed like a distant memory. 'The only way to not get tired is to keep climbing,' she said, as if it was my choice to not climb. I just couldn't. She also tried the 'pet dog trick' on me: 'Climb till here and I will give you a kiss/biscuit.'

The Himalaya though is kind and after every climb that kills you, there is a meadow/stream/view that revives you. In this case it was a beautiful straight path with the river flowing deep down below and a glimpse of the snow-covered peaks up front. But just the fact that the climb was over (for the time being) did the trick for me, and I replaced my stutter with a swagger which said: 'See, how I climb these climbs, ha.' The 'oh-so-experienced' Rujuta had a smirk on her face which I ignored.

Meanwhile, Gatuk, our guide, who had stayed back at Kafnu to load the four donkeys, caught up with us (let's not get into how much time he took to cover the same distance). 'Woh peak kaun sa hai,' Rujuta asked him. He smiled shyly and said in his characteristically low voice, 'Pata nahin.' 'Aur woh tree?' 'Pata nahin, hehe.' We looked at each other and decided that he was too sweet for us to feel bad about what he doesn't know.

Gatuk, however, had a good idea of distances and he told us to have our packed lunch right there as it would give us the 'energy' to reach the campsite. I was in no mood to read between the lines and sat down with my lunch box. Poori and aloo sabzi, a tasty combination at any time, acquires another dimension at moments like these. It's just the right kind of nutrients you need and it surely must rank as THE best option for a trek lunch. Anyway, good times don't last forever and we were soon back on our feet and walking.

The forest we were walking through was spectacular and incredibly diverse in the variety of trees, plants, shrubs and flowers, but the thing I remember most is that every single square inch oozed the colour green. I'd never realized before that there could be so many shades of just one colour: pale green, bright green, dark green ... my vocabulary is limited to these three only, but there were more than ten shades for sure.

As I rounded a bend I saw Rujuta talking with a man. 'You won't believe who he is,' she screamed, and without waiting for me to take a guess, continued: 'He is a government-appointed veterinarian. He looks after the merino sheep in the pastures of Kara.' You'll never find a job description that starts off on such a bland note but ends with such flair. Merino sheep in the pastures of Kara. Just say it aloud. 'So, you are from Mumbai too. I stayed there for two months while doing my internship and I hated it. You know why?' He didn't wait for me to guess either. 'The number of trees you can see here, in Mumbai I could see more number of heads.' We laughed weakly, realizing that ours could be two of the heads he despises. 'You guys will pass through Kara tomorrow – you must stop at our hut for a cup of tea.' Of course Rujuta agreed; she lives for such moments. And he sped away. This guy pretty much set the benchmark for 'amusing people you meet while on a trek' for us.

## *The campsite at Mulling*

The fact that our mind was taken off the vet within no time must bear testimony to the spectacular landscape we were now entering. For starters, the valley had opened up and there were flat patches of meadows on both sides of the Bhabha stream. The stream itself was not only visible, it was now right next to us with its water aqua blue and its flow swift but not thunderous. The mountain chain on our right was typical of the greater Himalaya – cloud high and rocky. The real fun was on the other bank though. The lush green grass stretched all the way from the river bank to a thick jungle of birch. A few wild horses were grazing there, the way horses must have grazed there of their own free will from forever. There was an unmistakable 'untouched' air about the other side, a kind of place that one is instantly attracted to. 'Udhar ja sakte hain?' I asked Gatuk. To our surprise he didn't say, 'Pata nahin.' He just said 'Nahin.' And added that there was no way to get to the other side.

Even as we looked longingly at the other bank, we were not oblivious to the charms of our side of the river. The hillocks had given way to a flat patch of grass right by the stream, and Rujuta was quick to pronounce it as 'a perfect camping spot'. Gatuk had a smile on his face as he declared, 'Yeh campsite hi hai' with a flourish, as if he had played a big role in turning the place into what it was. We could soon see our tiny two-man tent and the kitchen tent pitched up ahead and were already imagining Tshering brewing hot tea and perhaps even making some pakoras.

Limitation alert: Now, I must request you to turn to page vi in the inserts to see the photograph of our campsite and the other bank of the river as I am facing major issues in describing this place and have written, deleted, rewritten this part many times already.

Day 2 started early, for us at least, as we were up and about by 5:30 a.m. only to find all three guys still snuggled in their blankets in the kitchen-cum-sleeping tent. We decided to be nice and let them wake up by themselves. Wrong choice. When they had not woken up by 6.30, we had to do the honours. I opened the zip of the tent, stuck my head in and shouted for them to wake up. Obviously not very happy by this 'itna subah' wake-up call, they took their own sweet time to get up, do their ablutions and finally start the stove. By the time we had our omelette, toast and tea, put on our shoes, helped them with the tents and packing and waited for Lobzang to bring back the donkeys from the mountainside, it was well after 8 a.m. and we had arrived at a decision. No matter what, from tomorrow we would begin walking without waiting for them to wrap up. Anyway, they walk so fast that for them catching up is no big deal, but for us to start late exposes us to the sun for longer. Gatuk, feeling a bit guilty about making us wait, smiled and said, 'Today is very beautiful, most beautiful.'

## *The pastures of Kara*

He wasn't wrong. For an hour we walked along the stream, jumping over many smaller ones flowing down from the mountains on our right. Then we climbed steeply through thick bushes (shortcut) for another hour before reaching the most stunning pastures in the Himalaya. The pastures of Kara. So green, so wide, with so many flowers, so many sheep on the mountains on both sides, a small stream flowing in the middle and snow on the peaks all around. The trail also takes a break in Kara and you can walk as you wish. Looking up, then left, then right, then walking backwards, fumbling for your camera without taking your eyes off what they can see (photo on page vi in the inserts), and finally sending a signal to your brain to stop walking. Time may stand still at many places, but in the pastures of Kara it waits for you. It lets you make as many attempts as you want at grasping all the beauty of the Himalaya filtered into this one place. And then suggests you stay a bit longer by reminding you to have your lunch.

In a daze we ate, and then rambled on. An hour at Kara and we were still looking at it with the same amazement as when we first saw it. Our three guys were in their own world too, and so were the donkeys I guess as they were spread all over the pasture grazing on grass so nutritious, Lobzang told us later that shepherds walk from as far as 300 km so their sheep can graze here. Also, the government of Himachal has chosen this place to rear their Merino sheep in summer.

The mention of Merino sheep made us remember the vet and his invitation. Gatuk told us their hut was a bit off the route and we had already walked a kilometre ahead.

'Next time I guess,' I consoled Rujuta, and we continued on. But it wasn't going to be that easy to escape the vet now, was it. We soon heard some shouts and looked back to see the vet sprinting towards us, his arms flailing above his head, the king of Kara. And when the king himself runs behind you to invite you for a cup of tea, you walk an extra couple of kilometres. No questions asked. The hut was a temporary shelter made of blocks of stone and covered with plastic sheets, wooden logs and more stones. A fire had been lit inside, and it was warm. His orderlies brewed tea as he spoke and spoke.

I don't drink tea and at no time have I been happier about this choice. The tea they offered Rujuta was the typical mountain chai: so much sugar that the spoon stands on its own. Of course she couldn't drink it and tried to act smart by pushing the glass and exclaiming, 'Oho, gir gaya.' 'We have endless tea, don't worry,' and he poured out more for her. There was only one way to get out of the hut and that was to finish the tea. Heroically she did, and before he could download his three-month quota of talking on us, we were out, and waved our byes midway between his tenth story. I am sure he wouldn't have minded. We walked quickly till the hut was out of sight, and only the fact that it was Kara could slow us down after that. As we reached Gatuk, he was standing by a stream with his pants rolled up, sign for 'it's time to get wet'. The water was beyond freezing but luckily it numbed our legs in no time. Two more streams, then some vigorous rubbing of our legs and feet and we were up and about. Just take care of the occasional sharp stones and stream crossings can be a lot of fun. Or perhaps anything you do at Kara is.

We were now deep in the greater Himalayan range and quite high too, almost 3600m, and all the elements present at this altitude marked their attendance. Snow bridges, snow eagles, rhododendron bushes, windswept plateaus, all these and more accompanied us for two hours till we reached the high altitude meadow of Phushtriang, our campsite. At 4000m, it's amongst the highest campsites on a trek and presents a surreal scene. Huge glaciers flowing down from mountains on all sides, the stream flowing wildly through a rocky bed and green summer grass dotted with stones all around. You are never sure it's night at this height, as even the slimmest moon lights up the whole place. You want to stay out and stare, but the cold forces you inside. The mountains seem to say, 'You shouldn't have too much of a good thing'. So we obeyed and were in our sleeping bags by 7 p.m., ready to wake up early the next morning and climb the Bhabha Pass and cross over to Spiti.

This is what we discussed with Gatuk and Tshering before dinner.

*Us: We want to leave latest by 6 a.m.*
*Them: Blank looks.*
*Us: Give us something to eat before that and we will start walking. You catch up later.*
*Them: Slight hint of a smile and a nod.*
*Us: Show us which direction to walk.*
*Both of them enthusiastically: See, over there, that mountain. That's the one we will be climbing. There is a path don't worry. Just walk towards it and you will see the path.*
*Us: Okay, good night.*

## *The pass to Spiti*

The next morning was frosty but clear and absolutely still. It was bitterly cold and brushing, going for potty, etc. became herculean tasks. We somehow managed to do all that, ate something and were off by 6 a.m. as planned. In our minds, we were the two most determined people at that point, not realizing that just the scale of the mountains around us made us no more than two insignificant specks in the scheme of things. As we walked for about 30 minutes towards the mountain they showed us last night, fog started drifting in from whatever factories it's produced in the Himalaya. I mean, it's crystal clear one moment, then the first glimpse of the fog and before you can finish a sentence it's all around you. You feel that dampness against your skin, you can still see but you have lost the sense of where you are, your sense of direction. We walked like this for a further fifteen minutes and 'plonk' stepped right through the grass into chilled water almost till the shin. 'Wait, wait,' we both shouted together and stepped back. Water had gone right through to our feet and numbed them even before we could react. 'Arre, what is this?' 'I don't know.' 'Try that side.' 'You try.' Silence.

Eventually we did try and realized that it's the same everywhere. 'We are walking in the wrong direction ya, let's step back and walk towards the right. The mountain was on the right, right?' 'Umm, not sure, I think so. Let's try.' And we walked towards what we thought was to our right. 'But why is it so wet here?' 'Must be a snow patch which has recently melted.' 'Or the tip of a glacier.' 'No idea.' *Plonk*. We were shin deep again. 'What ya, I told you it's not this side.' 'No, you said, "you think so".' 'Let's go back to where we were and rethink.' 'But I don't know where we were.' 'That side.' 'You're sure?' 'I think so.' 'Please don't think.' 'Then you tell me, since you are the smart one.' 'Ya right, who got us here?' We fought as we walked in God knows which direction.

Let's do a quick check on the time. It was thirty + fifteen + five = fifty minutes since we'd left the campsite. Even if we knew how to retrace our path, it would have meant losing two to three hours on a day when the pass needed to be crossed. And we had no idea which direction we'd come from, which direction we had to go and where exactly we were. Once in a while we could glimpse the mountains through the fog but there was nothing we could make from that sighting. In fact, it only added to our confusion, with comments like, 'I remember seeing that peak last night. It was to the left of the pass.' We lost trust in each other's judgment, then in our own memories and finally in our instincts. We knew we had to calm down and just figure out what was happening, but we were not able to do that. Too busy feeling surprised, amused and scared that something like this could happen to smart cookies like us.

And then suddenly, 'There, there, look at that man over there,' we shouted almost at the same time. He was barely 50m away and was walking up a mountain. 'That has to be the trail,' we figured, and without thinking sped straight towards him. Was it to our right, left, straight or back, we didn't care, we just knew it had to be the trail. And sure enough, in less than ten minutes we saw a narrow trail winding its way up a slope. 'Wow,' we exhaled, relieved finally of the confusion. Rujuta was the first one to get her bearings and quickly took off her shoes and her socks to squeeze dry them. I did the same. We sat there for about five to seven minutes, and then started walking up. I mention the timing because I feel it's important to the story and not because I'm obsessed with it. Anyway, you be the judge.

It was a relentless climb now all the way to the top, as we'd been told, and the small zigzags built in the path were a great help to get our breath back momentarily. A couple of times I tried climbing straight up the slope, lost more time in catching my breath than what I'd saved, and thereon kept to the trail. It might be slightly longer but was surely the best way to climb. Turn diagonally left, walk four steps, stop, turn diagonally right, walk four steps, stop, repeat. Like two zombies we fell into this pattern and it was at least an hour before I turned back to see how far we had climbed. The fog had dissipated by now and we could see our campsite far below and even the tiny tents. It was a fantastic scene and worth taking a look at on page vii in the inserts, and also worth overlooking the fact that the team had still not left. Must be busy catching the donkeys we figured. It's good to look back once in a while when you are climbing up such crazy slopes to feel good about just how far you have climbed. Massage your ego and get back to the job.

On and on we went till we saw a crescent-shaped mountain wall up front, the kind of image we had of a pass in our mind, and high-fived each other. We struggled for almost half an hour to cover the short distance to the 'pass', the altitude was close to 5000m, but we didn't mind as it was 'the last climb' and from there it was all downhill. Just before we reached the wall we saw another one looming in front, higher than this one. So, it was not the pass after all; the pass was up ahead. 'Let's keep walking and finish it off,' I channelized my frustration into action, as the self-help books suggest. Big help it does. In five minutes I was pooped and was dragging myself, not even looking up at the new 'pass'. Another twenty minutes and no prize for guessing what happened. Yes, a new 'pass' up ahead. It would have been a joke had it not been for the absolutely stunning terrain we were walking through. It passed over patches of hardened snow, with more snow all around; some of it had melted and formed small ponds that reflected the snow peaks. Even if we didn't acknowledge it at that instant, such a scene is what makes trekking the unquestioned king of any travel mode in the Himalaya. One can justify any hardship for just one such glimpse; and just think, on a trek you are constantly walking through such scenes.

Okay, okay, no digressing, because we are approaching the pass and also the end of this story. After the second dhokha, we just sat there, forgot our obsession with crossing the pass as early as possible, opened our lunch boxes, took some photos and marvelled at the perfect weather we'd had since the fog. As we were on our second parantha we heard the familiar bell of our donkeys, signalling the arrival of our team. They hadn't even packed up some time back, and now they had caught up with us? How fast do they walk? Trust me, best not to think about it if you want to feel good about your own Atlas-like efforts. 'Very good, you are almost at the top,' Gatuk tried playing the guide role. 'Ya, that's great. We have been very close for a very long time,' we answered, disgruntled. But I must admit, the arrival of our team was just the tonic we needed and in their company we walked and this time without any apparent effort, we were on top of the actual pass. Stunned by our first glimpse of the Pin valley, Spiti. Photo on page viii in the inserts; please take a look before reading on. The guides did a quick puja at the pass, added a string of prayer flags to the many already present, had their meal, in which we also joined, and within ten minutes were ready to leave. Just the contrasting views from the pass as we cross from Kinnaur to Spiti tell you about these two places better than any book ever can. In the simplest of terms, we crossed from a million shades of green to a million shades of brown.

After a tricky climb down over a glacier for about 200m, it was a long descent over rocky moraine almost all the way down to the campsite, accompanied by the roaring and black Pin river. Baldar, at about 4000m, is a quiet, green patch with, as usual, a small stream passing through. We however saw all that the next morning. That evening, after walking for twelve hours straight, we asked Tshering to cook dinner for us straightaway, finished it by 6 p.m. and were in our tent and inside the sleeping bag by 6:30 p.m. We felt brave and safe, a wonderful feeling, another 'trek only' feature.

Now, here is the thing. It was almost eleven hours ago that we had seen that man. The man because of whom we'd found the trail. He was just 20m ahead of us, and not only hadn't we seen him later, we hadn't even thought about him till Rujuta said, 'Arre, but where is that man?' 'Haan yaar, I totally forgot about him. But he was only a bit ahead of us, how come we never saw him? We could see miles ahead almost throughout, especially from the top.' 'I know, even if he is a fast walker, he couldn't have walked that fast. There must be another trail I guess.' 'No, this is the only trail in this region. He had to be walking on this trail only. In fact this is the only campsite he could have camped at, but he isn't here.'

We were sitting up now, rewinding the day in our mind. 'And how come he was alone? You have to have a guide on this trek, right?' 'Yup, guide and porter and a donkey at least, even for the most experienced trekker.' 'So where is his team? Maybe ahead of him, but how come we didn't see them on such a clear day? We could see the trail for almost 10 km from the top.' 'I hope he has not gotten into some kind of an accident or lost the path. That's the only explanation I can think of. He looked so old and experienced.' 'What old, he was so young.' 'What are you talking about? He was an old guy, with a white beard and a walking stick. He was wearing a hat too.' Rujuta looked at me with her 'Don't give me bullshit' look. 'I'm not kidding. He was wearing a round hat.' 'GP, he was a young man with a backpack. Tell me you are kidding.' 'I swear, I am not.' We unzipped our sleeping bag, got out of the tent and rushed to the kitchen tent. Between quick gasps we related our story to our guys. They listened patiently, and then Gatuk told us matter-of-factly, 'Aapne bhoot dekha, sir.' ('You saw a ghost.')

## *Epilogue*

In May of 2008 I was at a nice, quiet retreat in the Kumaun hills with one of my first group trips at CWH. I couldn't believe my luck when I found out that Mr Harish Kapadia, the mountain man, was also there for a break. Over the next two to three days we got to interact with him a lot and at all times we pestered him for stories, particularly in the evenings when everyone sat around a small bonfire. He obliged by sharing his experiences and plenty of funny stories (he even gave a small talk on the Himalaya for our group). But people were specifically interested in ghost stories as that's the perception everyone had of the mountains.

He told us, however, that in his almost fifty years of travels in the Himalaya, from the remotest of valleys to the highest of peaks to the strangest villages, he has never ever been troubled by or experienced anything that is scary. 'The Himalaya is dev bhoomi, land of gods, so this is, in fact, the safest place you can be. But in climbing circles we use a term – the "friendly spirit phenomenon", to explain some of the unexplainable.' According to him, the Himalaya abounds with stories where a shepherd, a villager, a child, happens to meet you when you are in some kind of trouble – lost your path, or need shelter from a storm – and guides you to the right path or shelter. Only later, when you are safe and feeling secure, will you try to rationalize the situation and think of that person, where he came from, where he went, how come he/she disappeared just like that. The friendly spirit.

\* \* \*

## *Raju, the Guide*
*Short mein bole toh, the Pin-Bhabha trek is the best of the Himalaya compressed over four days.*

**More reading:**
Some easily-available books and guides I have managed to read and gained from:

| Title | Category | Author | Remarks |
|---|---|---|---|
| *Exploring Kinnaur and Spiti* (2002) | Travel and exploration | Deepak Sanan and Dhanu Swadi | The bible for this region. Few books can surpass the detail and accuracy of this one from the IAS couple. |
| *Spiti: Adventures in the Trans-Himalaya* (1999) | Climbing and exploration | Harish Kapadia | Some of the most daring explorations and climbs in Spiti. |
| *Himalayan Buddhism – Past and Present* (1993) | History of the area's religion | D.C. Ahir | If you want to read just one book about the history of Buddhism in Spiti and Ladakh, this is the one. |

## What else to do in Spiti

*Trekking* – You must go to Spiti and try your best to do so by trekking, either from Kinnaur (easiest) or from Kulu (Pin-Parvati) or even Ladakh (Parang La), although they are tough treks. Inside Spiti also you can trek from one village to another on high ridges, but they are not as dramatic as the ones where you cross a pass.

*Car/bike riders* – It's the next Ladakh in the making as far as the pull for bikers and self-drive cars is concerned. Don't make the same mistake of not understanding the effects of altitude (come via Kinnaur, leave via Rohtang Pass) and also don't just pass through Spiti as if you only came to see the road. Stay in a couple of villages and soak it in.

*Homestays* – Spiti Ecosphere runs homestays in quite a few Spitian villages and, as usual, they offer the most authentic experience of the life of the people, their food and their smiles.

*Monasteries* – Anyone with any interest in Tibetan Buddhism can spend months in Spiti exploring its monasteries, some large some small, but all with a wealth of information. All four sub-sects of Tibetan Buddhism are represented in this small valley and that is something no other place can match. Also, if you are hardcore and visit in winter, you will get to see Buzhens, the wandering lamas unique to Pin valley, who go from one village to another enacting the scriptures through easy-to-understand street plays.

**Point to be noted**

Kaza, the sub-divisional headquarters and also the capital of Spiti, is the only town in Spiti and also one of the few settlements along the river rather than high above it. My advice is to just pass through it, at the most buy essentials you may need from its markets, but don't stay there. If you want to stay somewhere other than a homestay, Tabo, with its Leh-like quirky nature, and also one of the oldest monasteries in Spiti, is a much better choice.

**Local service providers**

Spiti Ecosphere runs a wide network of homestays in some of the most beautiful and accessible Spitian villages.

They also help locals market and sell their produce and handicrafts. www.spitiecosphere.com.

If trekking, the best way is to hire local guides who will then arrange the equipment and staff. For Pin-Bhabha Pass, you should look for guides from Mudh village. Gatuk now teaches 'computers' in the primary school and doesn't have time to trek, but you can meet him when you are in Mudh.

For transportation, Sanjay Sharma, based in Shimla, is a reliable contact. 9816021966.

\* \* \*

## *Reality check*

**Kruti Saraiya**
**Teaches graphic design at Srishti, Bangalore**

(I did the Pin-Bhabha Pass again in 2011 and Kruti was part of the group. Here's her take on the trek in her words and drawings.)

*So when I decided to go on this trip with CWH, I had no clue what to expect, but I had been told by Rujuta that this trip is 'life changing'. While packing I almost had second thoughts about carrying a sketchbook and pens to a 'trek', but I thought if nothing else I might want to keep a diary about my life-changing experience; also that if the group was boring, sketching would be my saviour. In reality the exact opposite happened, the group was so entertaining with so many stories to document that page after page of ideas were just waiting to be sketched out. So these are not just pretty drawings – this is a full account of the trip with its drama, humour, stress, fatigue, gossip and of course the magnificent Himalaya.*

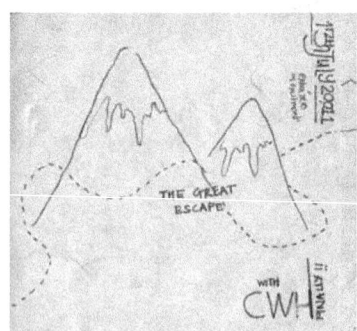
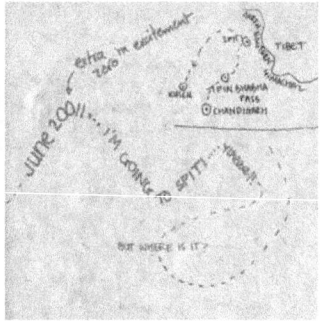
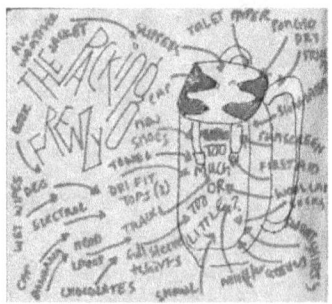

# SURREAL SPITI

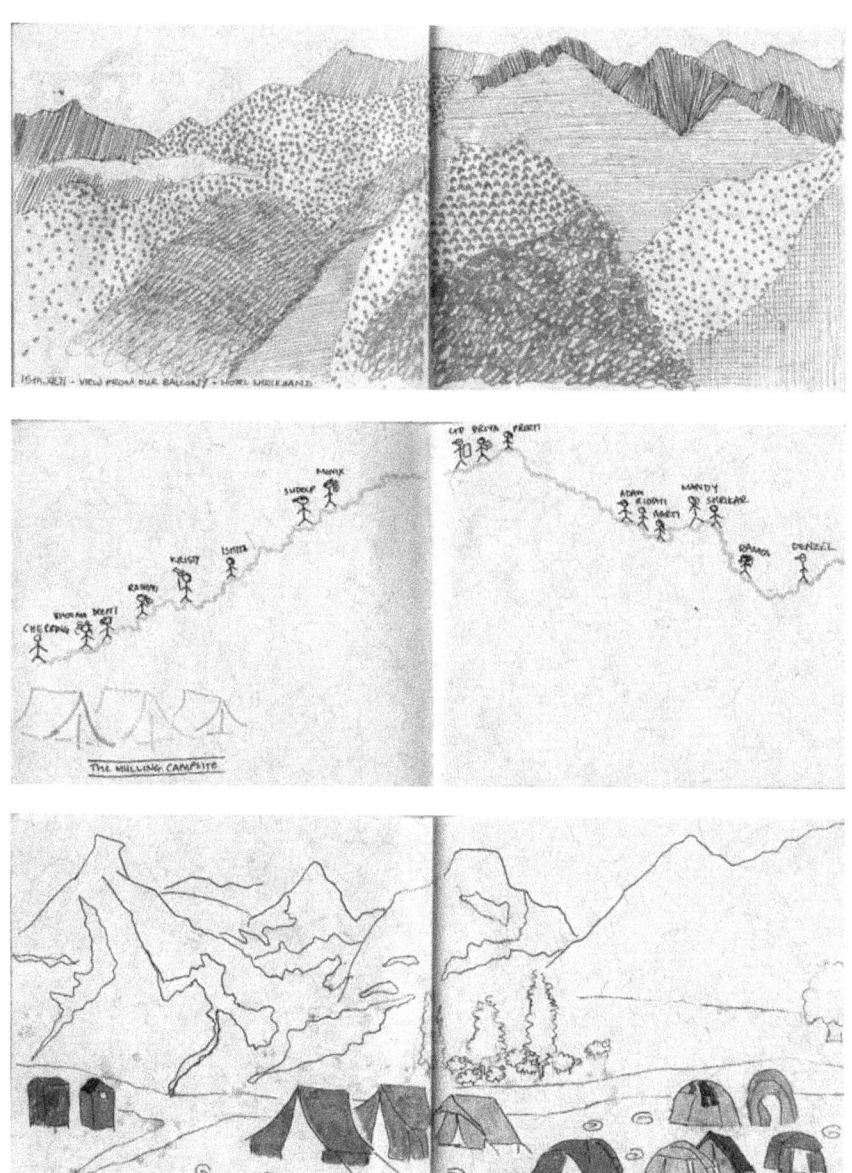

86 THE LAND OF FLYING LAMAS

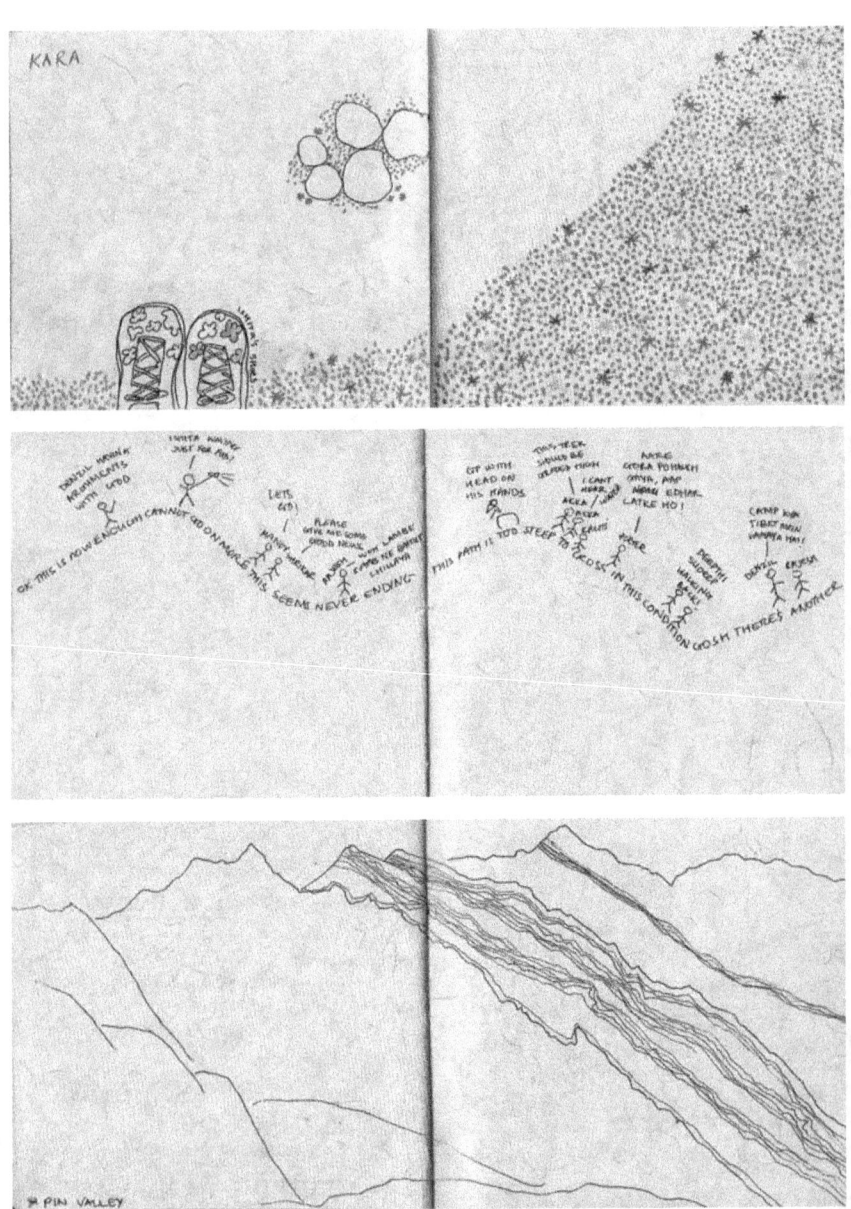

Vaccination time for this four-week-old Gujjar baby

The school in Lidder valley; each row is a different grade

Long lost siblings? Rujuta and the Chaupan woman

Time to avoid rock and just roll in the Lidder valley

When the going got tough, we got out and walked

How to capture the scale of Nubra with a camera?

View from the 'holding area'; we spent 2.5 days here

All's quiet as we climb towards Khardung La

Waiting for breakfast on a winter morning, Naggar castle

Krishna temple in the lost city of Thava

View of Kulu valley from Naggar

The first day campsite at Mulling on the Pin-Bhabha trek

All the beauty of the Himalaya condensed in the pastures of Kara

Climbing to the pass, campsite far below, dissipating fog

First glimpse of Pin valley in Spiti – worth the climb to the top

The tattooed women of Birthi

Our Day 3 campsite on the ridge between Rupin and Supin valleys

The morning after the snowstorm

The Pachi Thach, the meadow behind, the best there is

The trail along the Gori Ganga, cut through vertical rock

Just crossed the golden meadow

Waiting with bated breath for the unveiling

Lo and behold, the Nanda Devi twin peaks unveiled

Our homestay in Nagling village, just four hundred years old

The second meadow of Nagling

The walk on the glacier of the fourth meadow

The mystery of Nagling – where does this water go?

Food at Smrithi's place after the 10k run

With the Riverdale kids and Smrithi's family

A walk through the quaint Yuksom

The colours of the Dubdi monastery above Yuksom village

Story 5

# Rupin Supin – the Descendants of the Kauravas

Hand-drawn maps for representation purpose only. Not to scale.

## *The setting*

West of the Yamuna lies Tons, its tributary. Further up lie the Rupin and Supin, the Tons' tributaries. It is this region that has somehow fallen off the map – geographic and cultural. With the Char Dhams being the spiritual and economical hubs of Garhwal, the geographical isolation of this region, called Jaunsar-Bawar, is understandable. Cultural isolation, however, requires a dive into history – the mythological one that is.

'They' say it is those who win the war who write the history. The Bawaris would agree. For this is the land where Duryodhana and Karna have always been worshiped, where the natives claim to be descendants of the Kauravas, where, till date, local festivals celebrate the defeat of the Pandavas in a game of ball against the Kauravas. The temple architecture is rich, the traditions unique and the people very distinct. All ingredients worth preserving. But modern Hindu religion doesn't seem to have a place for such differences. Not since the serial *Mahabharata* beamed into every TV set and projected the Kauravas as mean, deceitful, conniving savages trying to deprive the brave, suffering Pandavas of their rightful inheritance.

The proud inhabitants of these remote valleys read the writing on the wall and en masse decided to keep outsiders out of their way of life. Spend a week with them and you will probably not hear the word Duryodhana. They will worship him as they always have, but speak of him they won't. If they are not sure about your intentions, they will even deny any link with the Kauravas. And why should they not do this. They are social outcasts in Garhwal. No government wants to be known as pro-Bawaris so they are practically living a century behind the times. Villages large enough to comprise 250 families have not heard of electricity, school, road or medical facilities. No NGOs operate here. No one speaks for them.

But there is hope. And that's in the form of sensible tourism. Treks in these valleys are amongst the best the Indian Himalaya has to offer. The meadows are huge and full of flowers, mountain peaks are all around and camping sites are abundant. From the recently mushrooming river camps along the Tons at Mori, one goes up the stream towards the relatively big villages of Sankri along the Supin or Tiuni along the Rupin. From either of these, there are countless treks to explore the entire region.

## *The stage*

High above the ridge separating the Rupin and Supin valleys lies a legendary lake, Bharadsar. Nothing surprising about this considering that the entire region is steeped in mythology from the *Mahabharata* period. As always, it's totally up to individual interpretation as to what's a myth and what's fact. Anyway, coming back to this lake. It's not easy to get there, I can vouch for that, and maybe that's why it is revered so much. Don't we always seek the unattainable? A trek starts from the Rupin stream and passing through the village of Birthi (or Bithri), with its tattooed women and poppy fields, takes you higher and higher towards the lake. It then drops down to Supin valley and its village of Pithari before reaching the road-head. We went in 2010 and were among the first few groups to go there, surprising considering it's so close to one of the most popular trekking trails in Garhwal, the Har-Ki-Dun, one of the horse-shit trails. So many people tread that trail with their teams in tow that once again I am not able to make up my mind as to who is to blame for not even thinking of going on any of the countless treks around the place: the trekking agencies or the trekkers.

## *The cast*

On a trek, it could be anywhere in the Indian Himalaya, you are accompanied by a guide, a cook and his kitchen staff, one of whom will be the extroverted type and will be the designated server, some porters and/or horsemen, depending on the suitability of the trek for mules or donkeys. Raju is not a popular name in the high Himalaya and the guides usually have more exotic names, in this case it was Swamiji. It's Garhwal, so there was a good representation of Rawats and Singhs amongst the rest of the crew, notably Tikam, the tough as nails, never smiling second in command. Not to forget the women and children of Birthi and Pithari villages. And a group of twelve of us novices.

## *The act: A village of tattooed women and surviving a Himalayan thunderstorm*

'Listen, it's just an 8 km walk today or what?' Sangita asked disbelievingly at the start of the trek. Somehow she never trusted me when it came to my distance or time predictions. Yes it was, but, as we were soon to discover, all uphill. The first day of a trek is always the toughest. It's when reality strikes and the romantic notions of walking in the wilderness are sidelined by the actual act of walking. Doesn't matter how many treks you've been on, the first day blues are unavoidable. And on this trek, the feeling was that much more exaggerated as we trudged uphill relentlessly.

The chatter gave way to grunts and soon the first round of complaints were whispered amongst the laggards. Ignoring them for the moment, I picked up my pace and went ahead of the group. The sun was beating down and as we were moving through a cultivated stretch of land, tree cover was non-existent. This is another big complaint I hear: 'I really thought it would be cold, it's the Himalaya after all.' But it's summer; when there is no breeze and no shade, it's *going* to be hot. Not to mention that the sun is sharper because of the altitude and clear air.

My water bottle quickly got over and as soon as I came upon a dwelling I asked the couple sitting outside for some water. 'Nahin hai,' the man retorted. Now this is unheard of. A remote Himalayan villager refusing water, and that too not very politely. I was still trying to justify this behaviour, linking it to what we have heard about the people from this valley being 'different' and often misunderstood, etc. when a young girl walking down the trail, jogging down almost, came upon the scene, admonished the man for not giving me water, took my water bottle from me, went inside and filled it herself.

Before I could say 'Wow', she had already told me that she was just coming down from a village where she volunteers to teach the kids, and she would now walk back to her village which is 7 km down the valley. Swamiji came by and said a very warm, and flirtatious, hello to her, which was responded in kind – they knew each other well. He asked her to join us on the trek. I was hoping she would say yes, but then she had to go home first she said, and would join for the next one. Oh, well. But her energy and radiance made my day and I am sure she is destined for big things.

## *A village of tattooed women*
The uphill trudge continued. I had checked on the first-timers during the break, especially Mushtaq bhai, who with his, how should I say this, bulk, was more susceptible, at least as per perceptions. But we didn't account for the fact that he lives and works in Himachal, and walking in the hills is almost a daily ritual. Rujuta's strength-to-weight ratio principle was at play here. Mushtaq bhai had the strength to carry his weight easily and that's all that matters. In fact, he turned out to be the biggest asset on the trek. He knew so much about the vegetation, why things grow in particular conditions, the peculiarities of trees and plants around us, etc., that walking beside him was akin to shadowing a walking talking Nat Geo channel. I, and a lot of us in the group, just absorbed all the gyan.

Just before reaching our campsite we passed the village of Birthi. As old goes, this one was right there at the top. Ancient is the correct word to describe it. The houses were of wood and a bit of stone, and were unique in their style and look. Passing through the narrow alleys of the village we could hear plenty of giggles and murmurs. Without looking up one could guess it was the village women amused by our clothes, our way of walking, our reason for walking, pretty much everything about us. Neeta was part of the group and so goof-ups were guaranteed. One came promptly. As she was panting her way up the alleys, resting frequently with her hands on knees, an old woman remarked in a clearly pitying and sarcastic tone, 'Bimaar ho?' That was cue for the rest of us to burst out laughing and seeing us do that the villagers warmed up to us.

We could only see women and children, lots of them. The features were striking, very 'different'. Women, especially the older ones, lounged in the verandas and Rujuta approached one such group. They were fascinated by her hat, her sunglasses, she in turn with their many piercings and tattoos. She requested them for a photo and they gladly accepted, posing, opening up the top buttons of their blouses to reveal their multiple tattoos (photo on page ix in the inserts). At such moments, the only thing that I can think of is how and when, as a society, did we let go off this openness, this bindaas attitude and become a less evolved species? Alas, satellite TV will soon come to this village as well and they will then 'learn' how women behave, talk and act from serials made in 'modern, progressive' India.

## *Where brides rule*

Like all remote Himalayan regions, Jaunsar-Bawar has been traditionally a very open and equal society. In fact, if we go by a

> few rituals, women hold a higher place in the scheme of things. Girls choose their grooms and he has to pay the bride's family money to compensate for their loss of an asset. Better still, divorce is completely accepted and in fact encouraged if the girl wants it. Of course, these customs are changing fast as the 'modern/progressive' culture penetrates the region.

When we trek, these are the moments you wait for, moments that refresh you, make you laugh, amaze you, take away the physical pain and leave you with happy memories. Passing through Birthi village refreshed all of us, even Sangita and Sarika, as they forgot to make their customary mid-day complaints, taken in as they were by the women of Birthi. To make matters better, just above the village we came across a sea of white flowers, all sprouting from the crop planted by the villagers. Mushtaq, our expert, didn't waste a second to tell us that it's poppy, harvested illegally by the villagers as no one from the government ever comes here, and it provides them with some much needed cash. Several of us, drawn by curiosity, picked up a few flowers and stems and were given a demo of how it's distilled down to its more potent, commercially available form. Out of scope of this book.

Soon we were at the first campsite. Ah, the joys of reaching a campsite after a few hours of hard trudging can only be compared to the best things in life: the arrival of your cousins to spend summer vacations with you, the arrival of rain in the last over of a match just when you are about to lose to bitter rivals, the ... okay I'm getting unnecessarily philosophical, but it truly is a special feeling. It was the same here as people who had been dragging themselves suddenly started running around barefoot, behaving like school children out on a picnic, finding their breath and voice and asking the cook for tea and pakoras. Friendly banter followed as everyone dug into their memories of the walk and took digs at each other for what they might have done or said while in an exhausted state earlier in the day. Typical campsite stuff.

The second day of the trek was easier, shorter and comparatively less eventful. We entered a thick jungle and walked all the way till the tree line, just under it rather, and pitched our campsite. I did notice, we all did, the scarcity of water sources on this part of the trek, for no apparent reason. The campsite was a nice opening in the upper reaches of the jungle and we could sense we were just a short distance from getting above the tree line where we would start seeing some snow vistas. So the evening was marked with a heightened expectation of the next day and the only noteworthy incident at the campsite was Atul's hilarious attempts to enact the movie *Shalimar* as we played dumb charades.

## *The ridge between Rupin and Supin*

It took an hour-long uphill trudge on the third morning to come out of the jungle and onto the fabled ridge separating the Rupin and Supin valleys. Just as we stepped out of the jungle and onto the ridge we heard the flapping of big bird wings and kind of guessing what it could be rushed ahead and luckily got a glimpse of the magnificent khaleej pheasant, the king of Himalayan birds and a very rare sight. We had come out just under an outcrop of rock called the Vijay Top, marking the start of the long ridge between the Rupin and Supin valleys. As we waited for the rest of the group to catch up, we were witness to the following conversation between Atul and Tikam, our strict, no-nonsense, second guide.

*Atul: Abhi kitna dur hai campsite?*

*Tikam: Bahut.*

*Atul: Yeh jagah bada acha hai, aap to bade lucky hain aap idhar rehte hain.*

*Tikam: (Grunts an 'hmmm')*

*Atul: (Desperately trying to win him over) Aapke liye to bada easy hoga yahan chalna.*

*Tikam: Aap log bahut slow hain, hum thak jaate hain wait kar kar ke.*

*Atul: (Grunts an 'hmmm')*

As Atul gave up talking to him, and the others in the group arrived, we resumed our walk, now more or less on a flat trail along the ridge. We were at around 3000m and the rhododendrons were everywhere, in fact both sides of the ridge were full of the pink rhododendrons flowers, interspersed with some other bright yellow and red flowers. It was quite an experience walking amidst this riot of colours and even the distant thunder and cloud build-up was ignored by all of us. I must not forget to mention that, due to the lack of stream water on this stretch of the trek, two porters were assigned to carry twenty-five litre cans of water all the way so we could fill our bottles directly from them. Their strength, stamina, and most importantly joy in doing this job was straight from the 'Karm kar, phal ki chinta mat kar' principle of the *Bhagvad Gita*.

We had left the villages behind on the first day itself so it was just us and the occasional shepherd with his sheep, goats and *the* sheepdogs. Every time I see these proud animals, going about their work without a bother, I unfairly start comparing them to their domesticated counterparts in the cities and they seem to be a different species altogether. A lot of people in my groups go 'Awww….' and 'Soooo cute' and all that, but they also know they can't treat them as they would a city dog: it's the sheer aura they exude. The Spiti incident, when we were chased by a sheepdog, is an exception, and mostly they just want you to move on with life and leave them alone.

Move on we did and finally reached the campsite perched on one side of the ridge with one trail continuing towards the Supin valley and the other climbing up to the Bharadsar lake. Since we were above the tree line, the site was pretty exposed and vulnerable to wind and storms coming from either side. A photo of this campsite is on page ix in the inserts. Our plan was to keep the next day as a day of options: you could either choose to stay there and rest or climb to the lake and back with the rest of the group. No point in forcing people to come for tough stretches on a trek when there is an option of staying put and resting it out. This way one gets to enjoy the trek and not become a victim of 'have to do this at any cost', where the cost sometimes is an end to your trekking career (not because of injury but just the sheer physical exhaustion that overtakes the intangible pleasures of trekking). So we had a discussion about this during dinner and roughly half of us decided to go to the lake the next day at 5 a.m. sharp, while the others would stay back.

## *And it comes*

Now, imagine this scene. It's deathly quiet on a moonlit Himalayan night. Half a dozen colourful tents are pitched on a ridge and appear from afar like little dots. The occupants are sleeping as comfortably as is possible at this altitude and in a sleeping bag. Slowly the distant clouds roll over, cover the moon and then the ridge and surrounding mountains. It gets dark, very dark. Soon, the first flash of lightning appears, momentarily lighting up the tents, followed soon by the thunder. Then the second, third and fourth, followed by drops of cold rain. The tent people are still snuggled in their warm bags, either oblivious to all this, or more likely, pretending to ignore it. With each round of lightning, the space inside lights up in the colour of their tent, orange or yellow. It's like someone is switching on a bulb for a few seconds and then switching it off. They turn around in their bags, slightly concerned.

Then the wind comes. There aren't any trees so it sneaks in without any warning. The tent cloth flaps, mildly first and wildly soon after. The rain, feeling left out, picks up the intensity and is now pelting down as hail on the tents, which now appear even smaller on this grand stage, insignificant props in a battlefield. The lightning, the wind and the rain, the elements are all revealed and the quiet night is anything but. The occupants of the tents are wide awake now, clutching their partner's hand or supporting the tent fabric, the millimetres of matter between them and the outside. Some of them call out to their neighbours, but soon realize that their voices are no match for the din created by the flapping of the tents. Depending on how one looks at it, it's exhilarating, scary or plain nuisance preventing one from sleeping.

From afar, if you could see through the rain and clouds, you would now see tiny figures moving around the tents, tightening the cords, piling extra stones on the anchors, checking the zips and shouting words of encouragement. They are the brave guides and porters, checking on each and every tent. Did I not tell you about the principle of karma they work by, rather live by? Just doing our duty, they would say nonchalantly the next day.

The storm rages, time loses its significance, the tent people make peace with their situation, some even try to sleep, and things take their course. Just when it seems like the storm has it in it to last forever, the distant glow of dawn appears and taking its cue, the wind slackens, the hail loses its sting and the clouds start to roll onwards for their next show, somewhere down the valley. It becomes quiet again, but the scene is very different. The storm seems to have left the colour white behind as everything gets a coating of hail and snow, the ridge, the tents, the mountains (photo on page x in the inserts). Disturbed by the sudden quiet, some of the occupants venture out of their tents and seeing the sea of white start jumping and screaming like prisoners on a life term set free unexpectedly after an overnight coup. Soon, the bitter cold of early morning brings them to their senses, and they, like others who already have, snuggle back into their bags. It's been an exhausting night being a silent and insignificant witness to a show put up by the elements, and they all need to re-establish their worth by snatching sleep back from the fleeting night.

\* \* \*

## *Reality check*

**Sangita Maheshwari (with Atul)
Commercial Manager, Lactose India**

*It was our third day of walking, rather climbing! At least that's all I felt I was doing! But anyway, we all reached the campsite at a respectable hour (read 4 p.m., just before it starts getting dark). Had our daily quota of chai and pakoras and debated the next day's climb to Bharadsar Lake. I was dead on my feet and had decided that I'd had enough. I'd climbed high enough to prove I could do it and now I wanted to spend the next day chilling (literally) while the more ambitious ones sweated it out to the top. I wasn't going to see the legendary lake tomorrow and found instant company in Sarika. She too was ready for a day of R&R.*

*After dinner we all called it an early night (not that we have any choice up there). In my tent I started having second thoughts... Am I just being lazy? Would I go back down and then regret not having seen the lake (that would have been bad as I simply wasn't going to walk back)? I decided that I would decide whether or not to go in the morning and drifted off to sleep. Only to wake up to the sounds of canons blasting! We were in the middle of a terrifying storm. The time was around 11 p.m. and the thunder and lightning were so intense that I actually began to wonder if the gods had decided to punish me for even thinking of not going to Bharadsar Lake! I was simply terrified (and trust me, so were the others in their tents). The fierce winds howled with such force that it was a miracle we didn't fly away in our tents. The furore just went on and on and on for what seemed like forever. A few hours into the storm, Swamiji (our guide) and the porters came out to check if we were all okay and we barely managed a squeak! Thunder rumbled from one end to the other and lightning lit up our tents every few minutes.*

*And then came the morning after. We got out of our tents at 6 a.m. to the most beautiful scene ever. Clear skies, a carpet of snow and absolute calm. It is a sight that will remain with me forever. Beauty in its most raw and sublime form. But one thing was certain – neither I nor anyone else was going up to Bharadsar Lake.*

\* \* \*

And so it transpired on the third night of the trek. The storm though, left behind a stunning morning and we gaped at the snow-covered mountains all around us, some of them being lit gradually by the morning sun. When the last person emerged from the tents and we all huddled around a fire started by the porters, it was already 8 a.m. There were sheepish glances all around, and no one mentioned the climb to the lake.

Swamiji spoke to me in whispers, 'Mushkil hai, it will be slippery because of snow.' I knew that, so asked him,

'Toh kya, seedha neeche chalein?' 'There is one more trail,' he remarked and seeing me sit up, continued, 'It passes through beautiful meadows and reaches the village of Pithari, and then the road. Very rarely has a trekking group been there.' 'Is it very pretty, worth spending two days?' 'Yes, it is.'

Armed with this new information I approached the group and told them about it. People were excited, relieved actually, that they didn't have to climb through snow or stay at this campsite any longer, and if the new trail was as nice and easy as I was saying, even better. So the decision was made and everyone dispersed to his or her tent to get ready for the day's walk. Paulomi though came up to me with tears in her eyes. 'Why can't we go up to the lake? It's so disappointing.' 'I know, but the guides are saying it isn't safe and I have to go by their judgment.' 'But then where is the challenge? I came on this trek to challenge myself, I have hit a plateau in life and in my workouts. This was supposed to be the time when I push myself out of my comfort zone. I can't believe this.' 'But we can't fight the mountains,' is all I could say. She will make peace with this situation soon I was sure, but I was reminded of how different our motivations and take-aways can be. Us humans, I tell you.

## *There are meadows, and then there are meadows*

Comforted by the thought of easy walks over the next two days, the group was in a happy zone and as we started the walk, everyone had their story of the previous night to share. There were plenty of exaggerations, additions and modifications of the facts, of course. Gusts of laughter and flashes of cameras accompanied us as we retraced our path a bit and then got on to the new trail that would take us to the most unexplored part of this unexplored region. The guides had called it 'a walk through meadows' and as soon as we reached the first one there was a collective 'Wow'. It was a small meadow, compared to what we were going to see soon, but stretched from the trail to the edge of the cliff and we could walk all the way to the edge and even look down. Since the walk today was a short one, this then became our lunch stop, and for some, a nap stop.

Meandering through open pastures we reached the campsite on a huge meadow called just 'Pachi Thach' or 'the meadow behind'. Facing the peaks of the Swargarohini and Banderpoonch range from right to left, and the glacier from which the Supin river starts, this campsite rivals the best known and exotically named ones in the Himalaya (photo on page x in the inserts). The happy zone we were all in was pushed up a notch or two higher just by being at this place. Everyone took off their backpacks and sat for a while, gazing in awe at the 270-degree panorama. The Supin river, a trickle as it emerges from the glacier right in front of us and then flowing down the slopes, was a breathtaking sight and a lesson in river origination few books can teach. Swamiji and Tikam joined us and told us about their climbs on the peaks we could so clearly see.

The next day was equally easygoing and the meadow where we camped was called the 'Badi Thach' or 'the big meadow'. It was incredible that such beautiful meadows exist so close to the road-head and are so untouched, unknown, unexplored. If not for the enterprising team of local guides we were trekking with, who had taken it upon themselves to promote their region as a trekking option and in turn earn an alternative source of income, no 'explorer' would have bothered to come here.

## *Duryodhana*

Just ahead of Mori is the village of Hanol and there resides Mahasu Devta, the reigning deity of the entire region. Duryodhana, after his travels far and wide in the Himalaya, came upon this region and fell in love with its beauty. He requested Mahasu Devta to give him the Bawar region and promised he would take good care of the people there. Mahasu Devta agreed and so Duryodhana ruled here for years. People loved him, and still do. There are temples to Duryodhana in almost every village, but the deity is kept at the main temple at Jakhol only, from where it's taken to each village. He is the final authority on any dispute and through a human medium (called maali) his spirit visits these temples and speaks to the

> villagers. (Similar practices are found in almost all higher Himalayan regions.)
> He was considered an expert in irrigation science and the sophisticated irrigation system used in these regions seems to bear testimony to this.

And finally we were on the last day of the trek and climbed down into the Supin valley and soon came across cultivation and other assorted signs of civilization. The villagers we met all knew our guides, in fact some of the staff were from these villages, and they excitedly exchanged news from the Rupin and Supin valleys. We descended into a big village called Pithari, equally old looking as Birthi and with equally good-looking women. As we all assembled in the village courtyard and were surrounded by the amused villagers, we were reminded of the reach of Hindi movies; a very pretty two-year-old girl was named Kareena, they all knew Mumbai was where the stars live and readily accepted our invitation to come and visit it. They don't even have electricity – how and where do they watch movies?

We soon bid goodbye to the villagers and continued our downhill trek towards the road. As I have often observed, the last day of the trek tells a great deal about who has enjoyed the trek and who hasn't. The laggards of the group suddenly find their second or third wind and rush ahead, whereas some have to be literally coaxed into taking the next step as they longingly look back towards the trail.

The sight of cars waiting for you at the trek end point and the subsequent ride, however bumpy it might be, is heavenly and the feeling nothing short of the exhilaration of reaching a campsite after a hard day's walk as I described earlier. Trekking in the wild, away from civilization, living without the 'essentials', altering the definition of personal hygiene, all for days on end, wouldn't be half as much fun and thrilling if there isn't the comforting thought of the car waiting at the endpoint to take you back to a bed, a bath, connectivity and eventually home. A quick group photo with the trekking staff, expression of gratitude through thanks and tips, promises to send them photos, and we were off to Mori by the river Tons. Trek endings are dramatically quick and so different from the starts.

Each one of the twelve of us in the group will probably describe it differently, and that's the beauty of trekking, the accumulated experiences, sights and thoughts are unique for everyone. For me, it was the thrill of trekking in a region with a unique culture, people and history, the experience of witnessing (and participating perhaps) in a full-blown Himalayan storm, the subsequent altering of plans and the luck by chance passage through the meadows. As always, Himalaya gives back much more than it takes.

\* \* \*

## *Raju, the Guide*
*Short mein bole toh, when trekking in Rupin Supin region, surprises come thick and fast.*

### More reading
Hardly any books exist in the 'easily available' category for the Jaunsar-Bawar region. There are some academic books on tribal ethnography and anthropology that cover this region.

| Title | Category | Author | Remarks |
|---|---|---|---|
| *Temples of Garhwal & Other Landmarks* (1994) | Culture | Rathin Mitra | A coffee table book, it covers the temples in the Rupin-Supin region in detail. |
| *The Abode of Mahashiva: Cults and Symbology in Jaunsar-Bawar in the Mid Himalayas* (1995) | Culture/ Academic | Madhu Jain | A study of cults and symbology in this region. |

## What else to do in the Rupin Supin region

*Trekking* – So many treks, but I will list one option each for all trek grades:

Easy – Kedar Kantha meadows is an easy two-day climb from Sankhri. In April, there will be snow on the higher reaches and later in summer the meadows will be full of flowers.

Medium – Try the Changsheel meadows trek for an ultimate meadow experience. You can either take a circuitry route and come back or continue straight and get out from the Rohru side of Himachal. The trek will take you about four to five days.

Medium-hard – The trek to Bharadsar Lake is a five- to six-day trek, with the toughest portions being the climb to Bharadsar and down. Also try and cover the mystical Vishkhopri meadow on this trek if possible.

*River rafting* – The Tons is a very kind river and lets you ride its rapids with ease. There are plenty of campsites in Mori which are set up during the summer months to do exactly that. They are a great place to chill too.

*Temple trail* – Go for a temple trail around Jaunsar-Bawar, starting from the Mahasu Devta temple in Hanol (all visits to this region must begin from here), to the Karna temple in Deora and finally to the Duryodhana temple in Jakhol.

**Point to be noted**

This is a great region for a holiday with the added thrill of river rafting, camping and history with its most interesting twists. From Mussoorie, it takes five to six hours to get to Mori, and making it as your base you can either trek around or just explore the area. Don't miss the excavated site at Lakhmandal (supposedly the site of the Lakshya griha incident from the *Mahabharata*) on the way to Mori from Mussoorie.

**Local service providers**

HMPA (Har-Ki-Dun Mountaineering and Protection Agency) is the name of the group formed by local guides and porters and – it goes without saying – should be the first preference for trekking in the entire region. They also organize climbing expeditions for those interested. www.harkidun.org.

Mori has the best boarding facilities in the entire region. They are all seasonal river camps along the Tons, operational mostly from April to June. Just google 'Mori camps' for details and contact information. No preferences.

Story 6

# The Mountain of the Elusive Goddess – Nanda Devi

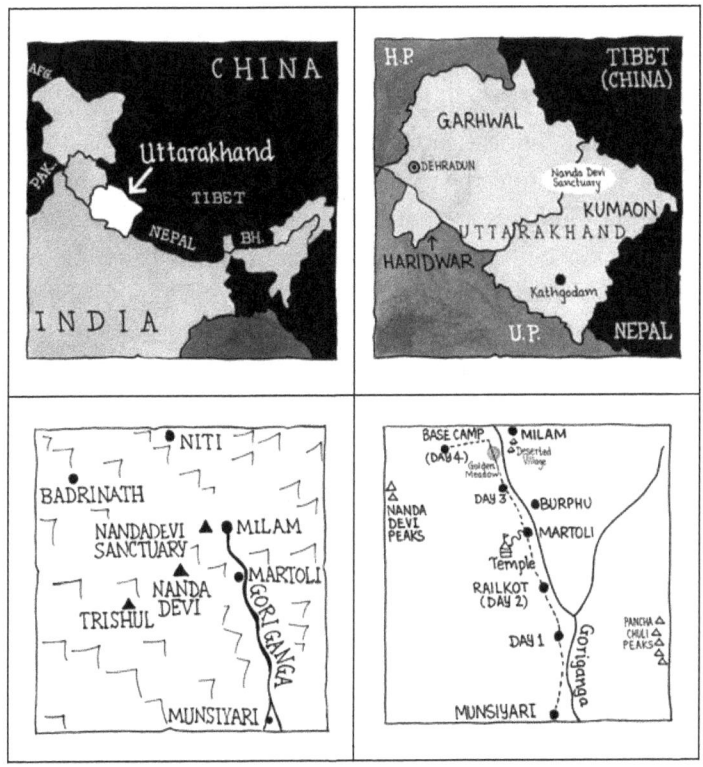

Hand-drawn maps for representation purpose only. Not to scale.

## The setting

Uttarakhand, that is Garhwal + Kumaun, has one of the most vibrant histories of any Indian Himalayan state. Even a summary is beyond the scope of this book. But what you should know is that it was all Kumaun to begin with before the British carved out Garhwal from it, and for reasons political and unknown, they don't like each other much. Even today, one of the biggest gaffes you can make is mistaking a Garhwali for a Kumauni or vice versa. If by any chance we have a Kumauni driver and we are driving in Garhwal, he will most likely tell the locals he is from Garhwal to avoid any issues.

But there is one thing which unites them, and that is the second highest mountain in India, the Nanda Devi, bang in the middle of Garhwal and Kumaun, and the residing Goddess of that mountain, whom both worship and fear. The Garhwalis stake their superiority on the Nanda Jat yatra that passes through it every twelve years (most interesting pilgrimage in the world, google it). The Kumaunis, not to be left behind, will tell anyone who will listen that the Nanda Devi east peak (it falls completely in Kumaun) is the *real* home of the Devi on account of its truer dome shape.

## The Nanda Devi sanctuary

In central Uttarakhand, on the Garhwal-Kumaun border, lies the Nanda Devi sanctuary/national park. In the centre of the sanctuary are the twin peaks of Nanda Devi, at 7800m the second highest in India (after Kangchendzonga), the undisputed Goddess of most of Garhwal and Kumaun (it can be seen from most of the villages, you see), and the mythological home of Parvati, Shiva's consort. The sanctuary itself is divided into inner and outer areas and comprises countless peaks (all above 6000m) surrounding the Nanda Devi and forming almost two impenetrable rings around her. I say almost, because nothing is absolute, we humans don't like nature keeping anything from us and will go to any limits to 'claim' what we feel is our right. And so, explorers struggled and struggled for years to enter the Nanda Devi sanctuary, then described as one of the last self-sustained biospheres left on earth, until in 1934, two really persistent ones, Tilman and Shipton, managed to enter the inner sanctuary via the only opening possible, the gorge formed by the Rishi Ganga.

They of course would never have imagined that their exploits (accomplished with a pure spirit of exploration) would lead to a mindless race amongst the rest to enter and see with their own eyes what a self-sustaining ecosphere looks like, paradoxically destroying the very nature of the sanctuary, cutting trees and hunting the tame bharal and other species to sustain their huge expeditions. Such was the greed that, in a matter of a few decades, almost all was lost and the biosphere could barely be recognized. I say almost, because nothing is completely destroyed, nature holds on with all its tenacity and bounces back at the first given opportunity. That opportunity came when the government, under tremendous pressure from conservationists, and perhaps after unsuccessfully dabbling with nuclear spying devices in the Cold War era (google this interesting bit too), shut down the entire sanctuary and so it remains, till date.

Before moving on, I want to share a very interesting observation about the sanctuary, which I first read in the superb *The Nanda Devi Affair* by Bill Aitken. Supporting the already well-entrenched legend that Nanda Devi is home to Parvati, is the satellite image of the sanctuary. The mountains surrounding Nanda Devi form a shape very similar to the Om symbol, and taking it one step ahead, *the* Kailash mountain in Tibet occupies the place of the chandrabindu above the Om. Hmmm, it's all very interesting and just adds to the very complex iconography and significance of this mountain in particular and the sanctuary in general.

## *The stage*

Johar valley, with the Gori Ganga flowing through it, is on the east of the Nanda Devi sanctuary in Kumaun and must surely count as the valley with the most interesting and tragic story in the Himalaya. At one time it was the main trade route between India and Tibet and the locals here had much more in common with the Tibetans across the mountain range than with those down the valley in India. In fact, natives from this valley were hired by the British in one of the longest and most daring spy operations ever (again, just google 'pundits of Johar valley' for some fascinating information). They were rich and prosperous from trade and also from agriculture. But as it happened with pretty much the entire stretch of the border between India and Tibet, the Indo-China war changed their lives forever, cruelly so. With trade closed, the proud Joharis had no option but to move down the valley and strive hard for bare existence. The villages were abandoned, farms left untended and within no time a civilization was uprooted.

So here we were in 2009, in Johar valley, in the district headquarters of Munsiyari, a village from which you get better views of the Panch Chuli peaks than even from their base camp. And if you are really lucky, you will be able to see a storm raging on the peaks obscuring them and then revealing them in brilliant glorious sunshine, within half an hour. All this before you have even had your breakfast. Munsiyari is rightly becoming a go-to destination amongst the off-beat places in Kumaun, and with careful development of sustainable tourism (as in, without disturbing the way of life but only adding to it), has huge potential.

Anyway, we are here because it's the last big village before the trek to the abandoned village of Martoli and the east base camp of Nanda Devi. There are permissions to be gathered from the local administration and the ITBP, both of whom insist they are not required but continue with the system anyway. This is also the place where we meet our trekking team and they in turn get all their supplies, load the mules, and so on. There is the usual hustle and bustle that all trek start points have.

## *The cast*
Ganesh, the guide, who made the mistake of wearing tight jeans, Vinod, the cook, and an aspiring stage actor and singer, women at Martoli, and our group of twelve, going for the longest trek we have ever been on (and most of us had never been on any).

## *The act: A never-ending day and the veil of the Goddess*

'Is there a trek which just goes downhill like this all the way?' asked Nikhil, rather wishfully, as we started the trek from Darkot by rapidly descending through the village. I smiled ruefully, my eyes seeing the enthusiasm with which so many of the group were walking down, but my mind calculating the effort and pain with which we will all be climbing this very stretch at the end of the trek in nine days. I admonished myself for thinking so far ahead, especially when the thoughts were not very nice. The verdict is still out on what is better: an easy downhill start and a subsequent uphill end to a trek or vice versa. I guess when you are on a particular trail, sweating and all, you will always find the other option better.

After a relatively incident-free walk – unless you count me losing my brand new sunglasses in the very first hour of a nine-day trek, Namita going through the day one blues and insisting her husband send a helicopter to rescue her, and us having to walk, one at a time, straight through a waterfall – we reached the erstwhile campsite at Rairgarhi that is now a site for a hydel project on the Gori Ganga. Like on so many treks in the Himalaya these days, the day one campsite here too was taken over by a ramshackle shanty where the workers stay, eat, do their ablutions, etc. Not a very pretty sight, but a pretty site nevertheless. The group was in high spirits however and we decided to sleep indoors, on charpoys inside a tin shelter, instead of pitching tents. They provided warm blankets and everyone was happy with the prospect of fun times with all of us in the same room chatting. The fun times lasted for less than ten minutes before everyone dozed off.

'Okay, so we have discussed this before, but just to reiterate, today is a long walk of 16 km to Rilkot, and unlike yesterday, you will all struggle, so be mentally prepared,' I delivered the 'thought for the day' during breakfast. But somehow I had a feeling that between the chomping of paranthas and slurping of tea, the words didn't quite reach the wool-covered ears. Earlier as well, during our pre-trek meeting, there hadn't been many takers for my logic of how a day with uphill and downhill walks in succession is more taxing than a purely uphill walk. Day 2 was going to be that kind of day.

Anyhow, we managed to leave the campsite at a good time, around 6:30 a.m., and started at a brisk pace – perhaps people were concerned about the long day after all. The bridge from awareness to action was yet to be crossed, however.

The Gori Ganga was in rage, flowing down at such a steep gradient with such speed that the noise of water crashing against rocks was deafening. The trail climbed along the right bank of the river and the sound and fury of water along with the strong morning sun sapped us pretty fast. After a couple of hours we reached Bogdyar, another small settlement and also a big ITBP camp. We had to show our permits and write down our names in their register, a break we all welcomed. One usually finds a soldier from their part of the country and such meetings with the army are always congenial and a showcase of regional bonding.

The group had automatically divided itself into three sub-groups based on walking speeds, and by mid-day they were spread well apart. Vinod was with the ones ahead, Ganesh at the very end and I kept myself strategically (yeah, right) placed in the middle so I could keep an eye on everyone. Before I tell you that I kind of failed in that mission, let me say that I did try, valiantly. Okay, so that's settled.

I always tell my groups before the trek starts that there are absolutely no issues in being slower than others and being the last one to finish a walk; in fact, that just means you have spent more time on the trail than others and will appreciate the beauty more. But that's easier said than understood. So here's a small attempt at recreating the second day's walk from the point of view of the last ones in our group, Somna and Anuradha.

## *The perspective from the backbench*

'These damn shoes hurt, and they are so heavy, and I spent five grand on them.' One of them – doesn't matter who – thought to herself. (All their conversations are with themselves, it's too tiring to speak, okay?) 'So, I have walked for two hours and as per GP's calculations, I should be done in another six hours, wait, that's three times the pain I just went through, noooo…' I am guessing not much appreciation of the scenery is happening, but a critical analysis of the trail is guaranteed: 'It's just going on and on.'

After Bogdyar, there was thankfully a flat stretch for almost an hour or so, as we followed the trail, literally cut through a vertical section of the mountain just a few feet above the river. (Limitation alert! Please take a look at the photo on page xi in the inserts.) It's a unique sight of course, but that was not what they were thinking. 'It can't be flat all the way. I wonder when the next uphill is coming.'

And then, 'Oh, I can see GP ahead. Is he tired? Is he waiting for us? That means the tough section is yet to start, oh no.'

So, playing Q and A with themselves, they reached the point where I was waiting, for all the three reasons above. From there, a narrow makeshift trail climbed straight up the hill, for almost 500m and then after curving around for some time, dropped straight down 500m. When I had reached there earlier with the group, almost everyone stopped just to look at it, wonder at it actually. Why would you do this to us, was the question in everyone's eyes as they stared at me. Luckily Vinod came to the rescue and explained that the original trail, which continued along the river, had been washed away recently and this was an alternate and of course much tougher route. But we had no choice.

So we decided to be brave, and opened up our lunch boxes – who knows what will happen later, might as well eat. I also decided to wait for the last group to break the news to them personally.

As I explained to Somna and Anuradha about the new route and showed them the trail, I was pretty sure they went blank. It was just the second day and perhaps a bit early for them to shout or curse me, so blanking out was the best option. (I was proved wrong about the shouting and cursing later in the day though.) I left them to their thoughts and Ganesh, and joined the group ahead. 'Well, I signed up for this trek, so I must suffer,' Somna and/or

Anuradha thought and opened up their lunch boxes as well, although they couldn't eat much. 'Maybe it looks tougher than it actually is,' they thought and started. And forty-five minutes later they just about reached the topmost point. 'I ... am ... dying,' even the thoughts were panting hard. 'But at least the climb is over, now looks like it's downhill only, and I am sure it will be easier,' they hoped, not able to listen to the knees screaming about what they were going to be put through.

## *The diet plate*

After the hour that it took them to come down the same distance that they climbed in forty-five minutes, they had pretty much given up on everything that's good in the world. And they had stopped hoping. While they struggle with existential dilemmas, let's take a quick peek at what's happening up front. The over-enthu crowd that rush ahead of everyone else at the start of the day usually get caught in their own trap and feel obliged to maintain their position as leaders. Every time they feel like resting or taking a break to admire the surroundings, or even take a photo, a voice rings in their head: 'What if he catches up with me' or 'No, I can't let the distance between us decrease', or some such useless thought. Trust me, do not envy the leaders on a trek.

After the steep downhill walk, the middle group reached the first of many 'hotels' we were to encounter on the way. (A hotel here is a tiny hut, made of loose stone, a tarpaulin roof and a dog as the security. The 5-stars have a wooden roof.) We would have missed this hotel if not for the leaders, Atul, Dimpi and Hitesh, who scampered out and rushed ahead as soon as they saw us approaching.

Once inside, it was cool, and tea and biscuits were served. The man running the hotel commutes from Bogdyar daily, how convenient, and is dependent on locals travelling on this route and the occasional trekker.

The diversion cost us more than an hour, two hours in some cases, without even covering 500m of actual distance. And it was not long before the question was popped first, 'How much more?' It was around 1 p.m.; a couple of hours had passed since we'd had tea at the hotel, and by the law of economics, one more hotel was due to appear. Voila, around the next corner, there was one, with an open veranda and two charpoys. It even had a blackboard with the menu on it: plate – 20 Rs, diet – 30 Rs. Must be a mistake, we thought, as we climbed up and crashed on the charpoys. 'Plate is only once, diet is unlimited food,' the owner explained, and we never found out if he was serious or whether it was his idea of a cruel joke on city folks. Diet it was for all of us and the rice and rajma we had there not only revived us and brought back our sense of humour, it gave me the strength to declare that we were only just mid-way. 'But it gets easier from here on,' I added quickly.

Calmed by the carbs and the assurance from the owner that it is 'seedha rasta' from there, we got back on the trail. We were high above the Gori now and almost around the tree line, so there was shade on some portions of the path and along with the refill at the occasional spring of glacier water, it made for happy walking. The valley too had opened up, and instead of the cramped up gorge, it was now wide open with high mountains on both sides, thickly forested around their base and with grassy pastures at the top. It's about this time when the Himalaya hooks you, giving more than a glimpse of what lies ahead, only if we keep walking and prove ourselves worthy.

### *The jealous Goddess*

Legends abound about Nanda Devi not taking too kindly to public displays of affection when in her realm. From the tragic death of a young climber when she paid no heed to the warnings from porters to not 'mix' with her fellow climber while on an expedition, to the gentle admonishing that Jahnvi received on our trek, the ire of the Goddess is well known. Soon to be married, Jahnvi and Nikhil were perhaps a shade too lovey-dovey on the first day of the trek. On the second day, as Jahnvi was walking ahead of us, on an innocuous trail, a small stone came flying from nowhere and struck her on her shin, instantly drawing blood. It was a minor cut, small enough for Jahnvi to be more concerned about her new tracks getting soiled rather than the bleeding, but it no doubt warned them off. On the other hand, Bhavana and Seema, who were travelling without their partners, conceived within a couple of months after the trek and delivered two vibrant baby girls ☺.

This was also the time when the last group, now walking in slow motion, started having serious doubts about themselves, about their decision to come on this trek, about me even knowing what I was doing, and most importantly about reaching the campsite at all today. One can only imagine what the mind does in such times to entertain itself. 'I have my jacket with me, maybe I will just lie down behind a rock and cover myself, and then in the morning, head back and somehow reach the road, hire a car and drive all the way back to Delhi, non-stop, and take the first flight home. Yes, that's plausible, isn't it?' Time moves slowly in the long afternoons of the Himalayan summer, or at least that's how it appears when you are barely able to drag yourself forward.

But for those of us walking ahead, the general feeling was that we were almost done and the supposedly tough day wasn't that tough after all. And just like that, as we turned a corner, we could see the ITBP camp at Rilkot, our destination for the day, in the distance and a collective hurrah was shouted. Distances in the high Himalaya are tricky though, and for us, unaccustomed to such scale, it doesn't make any sense when no matter how much we walk, the destination seems to remain just as far. In fact, it gets positively irritating. I tried telling everyone not to get overly excited, that it was still some distance to go, that the trail doesn't go straight as our sight does, it curves around the mountains and with all the ascents and descents it could take a long time, surely more than an hour, but everyone had been very patient since morning and now that they had seen it, the campsite just had to come.

Technically, it took us two-and-a-half hours to get to the

campsite from there, but by all accounts it was 'forever'. First the smiles vanished, then the frowns appeared, sarcasm and anger, in that order, weren't far behind, finally giving way to helplessness. What may now appear as irrational behaviour seemed perfectly in place then, with some people 'demanding' that the trail end and the campsite appear after the next turn, and some convinced we are on the wrong trail and shouting for others to follow them on a non-existent one. It was high-tension stuff, not of the 'last over and 8 runs to win' type, but more like 'will I ever get out of this'.

## *I accept, therefore I am*
If you guys are still with me, and still up for one last flashback, let's check on the group trailing behind. They had gone through all that the ones in front were going through now, more perhaps, much earlier in the day, and since the last time we checked on them were dragging themselves forward somehow. Unlike those ahead of them, they didn't notice (or more likely didn't bother to acknowledge) the campsite when it first became visible, and maybe that's why they had no expectations of it ending anytime soon. Like everything else, there has to be a rock bottom in this situation as well, and it came when one of them, doesn't matter who, threw up, sat on a rock and just cried, soon joined by the other. As the tears dried and nothing appeared to have changed, they got up slowly and started to walk again, somehow feeling lighter, more aware of their surroundings, more in tune, ready for what was to come next. In Anuradha's words:

* * *

## *Reality check*

**Anuradha Choudhary**
**Managing editor with Filmfare magazine**

*The first half of the second day passes without any incident. But by the time it's 3 p.m., I'm dead meat. As usual the seasoned trekkers are far ahead of me. Solitude turns to loneliness. I can't take a step forward. It's been seven hours since we've started walking and there's no sight of the campsite. I feel lost, depressed and am hit by a bout of self-pity. I sit on a huge rock and start sobbing. I curse God for not helping me. He's unmoved of course. A good cry does some good. But my body refuses to move and my eyes droop. The next thing I know is that Somna, who was behind me, has caught up with me. I'm done with crying and both of us, exhausted and emotional, get up to start negotiating the endless trail again.*

*That's when we sight it on the other side of the riverbank. The Great Himalayan Bear grazing by the river below with its cub. Suddenly, our deadbeat bodies stir with interest. We stop walking and watch the mother and baby. Everything is forgotten in that moment, in the sheer beauty of the animal.*

*It's God's way of apologizing to me, I'm sure. Apologies accepted and suddenly I'm already to negotiate the tough terrains once again.*

\* \* \*

I don't know if it was God's apology, more like a helping hand actually, but the crucial word here is 'acceptance'. Acceptance of the fact that they are out there in the wilderness, where the writ of nature rules supreme, one which can't be fought against, but only accepted. And with acceptance comes humility, and the ability to see beyond what you have been, whether it's a bear and its cub on the other side of the river, or a rare yellow flower right near your foot or the snow-covered peaks high above you. At that time however, the acceptance gave them just enough strength to finish the walk, well after the sun had set and the cold had crept in.

Their smiles as I met them on my way back from the camp with some tea and warm clothes took me completely off-guard and I fumbled with my well-planned speech about, 'it's okay, you have done great, don't panic, the extra distance offset our calculations, etc. etc'. 'We saw a bear,' is all they said, which ideally should have brought tears to my eyes after all the gaalis I had just heard from everyone else, the supposedly fitter and faster members of the group. I gave them some tea to drink, a biscuit to eat, a shawl each to wrap themselves in and the three of us walked back to the camp in silence; a relaxed, calm walk, savouring the sound of the river and the sight of a splendid dusk, the way it ought to be.

## *But we don't learn that easily, do we?*
One can only imagine that a nine-day trek would give people enough time for this crucial lesson to be reinforced. After that fateful Day 2, where we ended up walking almost twelve hours, not just our minds, but the entire Himalaya opened up and welcomed us big time. For the next two days we walked in a postcard, passing through huge green meadows with all kinds of flowers, sheep grazing lazily and snow reflecting from the peaks in every direction. A Lammergeier (Himalayan eagle) scooping down to pick up a lamb would have kind of spoiled the picture, but luckily it missed as the sheepdogs chased it away just in time. Everyone in the group was in great spirits now and comments like, 'This is what I am talking about' were heard with regularity.

On Day 3, as we walked through the open pastures, we reached the village of Martoli, the first of the trio of trading villages in the Johar valley, almost deserted, with roofless homes (the wood in the roofs was used as fuel long ago by the army) like the other two. The village was exceptionally pretty as it was located bang in the middle of a green pasture, right under the historic Traill's Pass in the east, the beautiful peaks of Trishuli and Hardeol in the north, and the Gori flowing down below. We were to stay for a full day in this village on our way back, so wanting to reach the campsite as soon as possible (yesterday's wounds were still fresh) we had a quick lunch and walked on, not paying heed to our guide's suggestion to visit the local temple dedicated to Nanda Devi, high above the village. 'We will see it on the way back. We are staying here anyway, right?'

On the other bank of the Gori Ganga we spotted the village of Barphu, stunningly nestled between mountains and sitting beside a stream. It has many more residents, its operational watermill a proof of that. (Refer 'Vinita Hoon' at the end of this chapter.)

We were now just one day away from the Nanda Devi east base camp and the excitement was palpable. Vinod and Ganesh fanned it further by giving a graphic description of how close the peak is from the base camp: 'You can open the zip of your tent and touch the peak.' The next day's walk first took us through a meadow of golden grass, yes, golden (and the photo is on page xi in the inserts), and we continued on till we reached a big stream flowing from the left. It was all too grand for us to even comprehend; besides all we were concerned about was how to keep the sharp and biting wind out of our ears. Across the Gori we could now see Milam, the largest and most important village in Johar. Our path, however, was along the stream on our left and we decided to take a break before starting on the last stretch.

This is what we remember of the last stretch: it first climbed up through a thick forest of birch and then white rhododendrons, then suddenly the clouds came and it started to drizzle, which soon graduated to hail and we covered ourselves with our jackets and ponchos, our noses froze, the terrain gradually changed from green to rocky moraine, we had to climb down the slopes of small side streams and then scamper up the other side, we huddled up during a break in the hail and ate our lunch, and lastly the hut of a shepherd which we all gate crashed into because he had a fire going. Phew.

'Okay, so how much further to the base camp and the view of Nanda Devi mountain?' asked Hitesh, caressing the big SLR around his neck, which he had lugged all the way, along with a tripod, just to take a photo of Nanda Devi from the 'closest distance possible'. 'We are already there, that ground over there is the base camp,' Vinod replied, and Hitesh's and most of the others' reaction was to be seen to be believed. 'But where is the mountain?' 'It's right there, but we can't see it because of clouds and fog.' 'But we have walked for four days to get here,' voiced some and thought the rest. 'Let's hope it clears in the morning. But you should all be proud of the fact that you have reached the base camp, walked for four days, climbed from 1800m to 3500m, braved the sun, wind and snow – it's really something,' I said and looked expectantly at the group. 'What's the guarantee it will clear up in the morning?' was all that I got. 'Let's hope,' was all that I gave back.

One could have easily wagered on what would happen in the morning – yes, no view. Nanda Devi was less than a kilometre away, but chose to stay behind a veil, a veil of nothingness, but one that was completely opaque. But a good night's rest and the realization that the tough part of the trek was over and the return would now start, plus a hearty breakfast of course, ensured everyone took a philosophical stand about this. 'But see, we are camped right under Nanda Kot peak, we can see the Nanda Devi east glacier right in front, all around us are grand mountains on a grand scale, we should be happy.' It was true, the place was out of this world. We were on the periphery of the Nanda Devi sanctuary, and even though we couldn't see the peak, we could sense her presence. All in all, we were overwhelmed, and unburdened, and with that feeling started our journey back, a journey filled with much more laughter and much more appreciation of the place we were walking through.

## *The veil is lifted*

Back in Martoli, as we loitered in front of the hut where we stayed, some lying out in the sun in their sleeping bags (it was windy), some reading books that they'd carried all the way, everyone trying to get used to the feeling of not walking after five days, we could see a big group of people, but not trekkers, locals, heading towards the Nanda Devi temple. 'It's a special day and these people have walked all the way from Munsiyari to do a puja in the temple. You should come – there will be some very tasty local food,' we were told and that was enough to make us climb up on a rest day.

The temple is some twenty minutes above Martoli village and is quite old, with some really intricate wood carvings, short walls but very wide with a slanting slate roof, and a huge compound. 'Why have they made the temple so high and far from the village?' Atul asked out loud to no one in particular. 'Yahan se Nanda Devi dikhti hai,' replied the priest, pointing to the direction where Nanda Devi was still hidden behind clouds.

> ## The atheists
>
>
>
> Every time we visit a remote village and go to its temple/monastery/shrine, invariably some of the group members will maintain a safe distance and not enter. I completely understand where that is coming from of course, but the difference here is that a temple or any place of worship in the remote Himalaya is much more than a room for an idol. It's the epicentre of the village, its cultural hub and – most importantly – an unrivalled peek into its past. The architecture, till it's defiled by standardization, is the stamp of that region and probably the last place that it exists in its pure form. Not interested in architecture? Okay, what about the stories? There isn't a temple that doesn't have an associated story, not a supernatural type but a practical one, which explains the psyche and beliefs of the natives. And that usually is the history of the place in a nutshell. So here's some advice: leave your coolness behind and go inside.

After praying in the temple, the group sat for the prasad and so did we. And what a prasad it turned out to be: a bhaji, thick red rice, poori, a local dal with some rajma and topped with halwa, all made in a unique way, but made so well, in desi ghee and all. We could barely lift ourselves from the ground, walking unsteadily to put back the plates and then to wash, and as soon as we were done, someone shouted, 'Look the clouds are lifting.' I'm not kidding, but the layers were coming off, and we just knew it was time. 'Climb up a bit more for the best view,' we were told and we did, to the birch forest above the temple, and then we all sat, looking silently towards the mountains, all mesmerized by the show Nanda Devi was putting up (photo on page xii in the inserts). Over the next forty-five minutes, every single cloud floated away, and one by one, the twin peaks of Nanda Devi gracefully came out in the open.

Long after we had exhausted our fingers clicking photographs, and our feet standing on the slope of the hill, and our brains trying to identify all the other mountains we could see, and even when the sun started to go down, and the chill forced us to huddle close, we remained there. We didn't need the villagers to tell us later that such a clear view is possible only once a month; we knew we'd gotten lucky, perhaps because we finally visited the temple and paid our respects, or because we overcame our disappointment on not seeing the mountain from the base camp and 'accepted' what we'd received, or just because we were at the right place at the right time – the reasons didn't matter. What mattered was the sight of two golden triangles rising above everything else around them, and us able to savour it for as long as we wanted to. (Photograph on page xii in the inserts for you too; you read this long account after all.)

\* \* \*

## Raju, the Guide
*Short mein bole toh, trekking around the Nanda Devi sanctuary is the closest you can get to a 'spiritual' journey.*

### More reading
Some easily-available books and guides that I have read and gained from:

| Title | Category | Author | Remarks |
|---|---|---|---|
| *The Nanda Devi Affair* (1994) | Travelogue | Bill Aitken | An ode to the mountain and its mystique, unlike anything else available in a book form. |
| *Nanda Devi: Exploration and Ascent* (2000 reprint) | Exploration/climbing | Eric Shipton and H.W. Tillman | The authors describe their explorations that lead to their being the first people to ever enter this sanctuary. |
| *An Eye at the Top of the World* (2007) | Espionage | Pete Takeda | Well, who doesn't like conspiracy theories. |

### What to do in Johar valley
*Trekking* – Essentially, you can go on this trek. But luckily, there are many options within this trek and you can choose to do a shorter version where you stop at Martoli, or the

one to a lake above Bogdiyar, only known to the locals and supposedly 'out of this world' pretty. From Munsiyari you can also go to the meadows of Khaliya, a short 8 km hike, but with some of the best views of Himalayan peaks stretching from Nepal to Garhwal.

*Chilling out* – Munsiyari is a superb option to chill out, provided you don't mind the long drive to get there. But again, break up the drive over a couple of days and you will really enjoy that part as well. Around Munsiyari, you can go for countless short walks, visit local handicraft stores or just stare at the Panch Chuli peaks.

**Point to be noted**

Munsiyari is home to two very interesting personalities. Dr Pangti, or Masterji as he is popularly known, is amongst the last surviving Joharis who used to be involved in trade with Tibet. He maintains a small 'museum' of photographs, documents and some other interesting relics from those days.

The other one is Malika Virdi, a mountaineer and social worker who decided to make Munsiyari her home. She was elected sarpanch of the van panchayat and works towards women empowerment. She runs homestays in Munsiyari and can be reached at malika.virdi@gmail.com.

I must also mention Vinita Hoon, an environmentalist and author of *Living on the Move*, a book on the nomadic tribes of this region. We met her on our way back, and as Atul tried to tell her, 'You have almost reached', she replied with 'Yes, I know, it's my twenty-fourth time'. She was working in Barphu village and helping them set up a water mill. Some women are truly exceptional, and she is one of them.

### Local service providers

If you want to trek anywhere in this region, get in touch with Ganesh Singh, a local guide (our guide on the trek) who – apart from organizing everything that you might need – is a very insightful pair of eyes on the trek itself. His number is 9456721651.

Another useful contact is Parminder Sethi in Kathgodam, the railhead, for all your transportation needs. 9410588889.

To stay: Try the homestays run by Malika Virdi or for the more luxurious option, the resort by Wayfarers.

Story 7

# Darma Valley: The Land of Flying Lamas

Hand-drawn maps for representation purpose only. Not to scale.

## *The setting*

When the chapter (and the book) is named as exotically as 'The Land of Flying Lamas', I think it's sensible to start with that. We didn't see any flying lamas, but we were with one. And here is his story:

A child was born in one of the three sister valleys in one of the remotest corners of the Indian Himalaya – the border of Kumaun, Nepal and Tibet. Along with everything else, the culture and traditions here were a unique combination of Tibetan Buddhism, nature worship and Hinduism. The holy men were called lamas, but they prayed to trees and rocks, using rituals not very different from Hindu priests.

The child was special, his parents could tell from his extra bright eyes and calm demeanour. And soon enough, senior lamas of the three valleys knocked on their door, looked at the child and unanimously declared that he was the reincarnation of a very learned lama from the distant past. When he turns five, his education will start, they told his parents and left.

On his fifth birthday, the parents waited for the lamas to come and take him away for his education, but no one came. Confused, they asked their son if he knew anything about it (he was a higher being after all). 'My education has already started,' he said. When? How? 'I learn at a big monastery.' Huh? 'In Lhasa.' Silence. 'In my dreams.' Stunned silence.

It appeared that the lama was learning the ancient scriptures from famous lamas, all in his sleep. His specialty was herbs and natural remedies and his mandate was to help the people of his three valleys in case of sickness and injury. And he was given a special power to reach where he was needed – the power of flying.

Cut to 2008 and our trek to one of the three valleys – Darma valley. We were amongst the first few 'non-explorer', 'commercial' trekkers there and who do we get as our guide – the flying lama. From the moment we met him, without the baggage of his story, we felt something special about him; the way he talked, calm and in control always, the twinkle in his eyes, and most of all, the respect he commanded from everyone without once demanding it. 'This is Lamaji, a very special person, and you guys are lucky he has agreed to come along with you for the trek,' we were told.

On the first night of the trek, as we all sat outside and talked, the porters told us his story. 'So you are saying he can fly?' asked Esha, the bright sixteen-year-old in the group, with enough sarcasm to drown the three valleys. 'Have you ever seen him fly?' 'Yes, I did, once. He was sitting beside me around a bonfire and before I knew it he was on the other side. He just flew.' 'Can he show us by flying from here to there?' Esha was relentless. The unperturbed lama had a constant smile on his face. 'Lamaji, show them,' the porters asked, obviously hurt by the tone used by us non-believers. Lamaji continued to smile.

Day 2, as we climbed higher, Kinjal started getting a headache and felt very, very tired. Lamaji ran up (or did he fly?) the slope, plucked a few leaves from a plant, came down, rubbed it in his hands to make a small ball and asked her to eat it. 'It'll help your breathing,' he told us. 'Must be a herb which dilates the capillaries,' Rujuta reasoned. Within half an hour Kinjal was feeling better and all of us, feeling a bit left out, wanted to taste the miracle medicine too.

That night we reached the village of Nagling and in addition to the five porters there was the entire village to corroborate the story. As all of us stepped up the pressure on him to fly, he finally told us this: 'I have never stepped out of the three valleys, but I can describe each and every detail of Lhasa, the monasteries, the roads, everything. It all happened in my dreams. I learnt the scriptures when I didn't even know how to read. I was given the power to go from one place to another in case of extreme emergency. It's not to show off. One time I was careless and I decided from then to stop my practice.' And he smiled again.

That's his story and regardless of what we or you, the reader, feel about it now, in that moment, in that village far far away, beyond civilization as we know it, amidst four-hundred-year-old homes, below the snow-covered peaks lit by the moon and high above the shining waters of Dhauli river, all of us felt if ever there was going to be a person who could fly, it has to be this lama in Darma valley.

## *The stage*

It was June 2008, and we were on a trek to the base camp of the Panch Chuli peaks, passing through the Darma valley. It's a very doable six-day trek back and forth from the nearest town of Dharchula. Nagling is the biggest village in the valley and an important stopover on the trek. It's a village that redefined old for us. The 'homestays' we spent the night in were stone houses at least four hundred years old. They were basic with small rooms and even smaller windows (to protect against the cold). And this was the 'palace', so imagine the rest of the homes. (Photograph on page xiii in the inserts.) But it was inhabited, which can't be said of so many old villages this far up in the Himalaya. Like all villages on the Indo-Tibet border, the people here were bitter about the abrupt stop to trade and their way of life. They proudly told us, 'Before 1962, when the army came here, we didn't even know what India was. We had our own currency and our own laws.'

The day we reached Nagling village, the entire population was gathered around a goat (which had died of old age); it had been cut up in the courtyard and different body parts were being distributed to each family. Later in the evening they told us that tonight was the scheduled visit of the 'Big Man', a seven foot creature who visits once every week in the middle of the night to check if all is well and punish those who did any wrong. We had a fitful sleep and some of us even heard (imagined?) footsteps outside our room.

We trekked for two more days to reach the base camp, had a great time there and on the fourth day were back in Nagling.

## *The cast*
Lamaji, our guide, the three girls in the team as part guides-part cooks-part friends, Nagling inhabitants and our group of eight, five of whom were on their first trek ever.

## The act: The four meadows of Nagling and the Himalayan Viagra

'But abhi aapne kuch dekha hi kahan hai?' Lamaji said and yes, smiled at us.

We were having our dinner in the open-air veranda in Nagling village, high above the Dhauli Ganga, and in line with the peaks all around us. Nagling was like our second home by now; we had spent two days there and seen all there was to see: a goat being cut and distributed amongst the villagers, a close encounter with the resident zombie, a volleyball game with the locals, and a high energy song and dance routine in the night. But Lamaji, our guide, the three girls of our trek staff and everyone in Nagling felt we were yet to see the real deal. 'Kisi ko pata nahin hai,' Lamaji said in hushed voice, and went on to tell us about the four meadows of Nagling. All different from each other, all unique, he insisted. We were all ears.

We had been trekking in Darma valley for the last four days and it had already surprised us, amazed us rather, beyond our wildest imagination. We were convinced there was nothing like this anywhere, and now these four meadows ('bugyals' in the local language) seemed like the last great surprise in the Indian Himalaya, and we the chosen ones to go see them. Trekking is known to induce delusions of being path-breaking explorers.

And so it was decided that instead of heading straight back to the campsite at Urthing, we would get up early and climb up to the four meadows, return by lunch and continue to Urthing. A long day, but we were sure it would be worth it. Lamaji had said so, and if a person who can fly is giving his word, we better believe it.

The night passed by without any visit from the Big Man this time, anyway he only visits once a week, and we were all up and ready by 5:30 a.m. The sun as usual had beaten us and we could see the top of the Nagling peak shining in the morning sunlight. We had a quick breakfast of omelette and toast, and with Lamaji leading us started the climb to the meadows. This also turned out to be the steepest climb of the entire trip and within half an hour we were panting and sweating and collapsing. Before we could revive ourselves, we heard sounds of raucous laughter and looked back to see a group of Nagling women climbing up with baskets on their backs, obviously amused by the sight of our group – some sprawled over rocks, some on their haunches, some barely able to open their eyes from the sweat running down their faces. 'Ruk ruk ke aao,' was the advice given, as if we had never considered stopping to breathe as an option.

The women, who were going to the meadows to collect fuel wood, herbs and flowers cheered us up with the songs they sang while climbing up and as we recovered urged us to follow them. Which we did, but just for five minutes, and told them to go ahead, we will come, ruk ruk ke.

Anyway, after about fifteen more minutes, Lamaji announced the climb was over, always the nicest thing to hear on a trek. We had been climbing through a thick forest and were now almost above the tree line, with the forest giving way to flattish terrain. It was just 6:30 a.m., but the day was already in its full glory, with birds chirping, flowers blooming and the sky acquiring a deep blue. 'Just ahead is the first meadow, the meadow of Kasturi mrig,' announced Lamaji. He told us that the grass that grows here attracts the musk deer and that they come here all the time to graze. They weren't there at that time though, it would have been too much anyway. One of the rarest animals in the world, the musk deer is almost a mythical creature now, found more in stories than in reality, and it felt special to stand on the grass where one of them could have been grazing just last evening.

'Okay, and what's special about the second meadow?' the impatient Kinjal wanted to know. 'Sabse sundar hai woh,' was the short reply, enough to get us moving. As we walked, the valley started to open up, the trees disappeared, the sound of flowing water was heard and almost like magic we were staring at the 'sabse sundar' place we have ever seen. Honestly. I have to put in a limitation alert here: just don't have the capability to describe it. First take a look at this photograph on page xiii in the inserts, before I even try. Straight in front was the Nagling peak covered with snow, a stream, obviously coming from the snows, was gurgling by our left, we were walking on a flat ground which stretched for almost half a kilometre to our right and which was covered by so many flowers, like a green canvas randomly sprinkled with every single colour possible. In the middle of the meadow, the women were walking in a straight line whistling some song and, wait, you get the idea right, it was basically a sensory overload. We did the only thing we could have done: just sat there and looked around. Lamaji had an 'I told you so' smile on his face and was on a high too. 'We are not moving from here,' Jahnvi and Nikhil declared, no one argued, and no one moved.

After fifteen minutes of aimless sitting around, we decided to 'utilize' this time better and opened our lunch boxes. It was early for lunch, but anything to spend more time at this place. We shared the meadow with the cattle of Nagling village. During summer, they are left to graze here on their own for two to three months. More than a few of us eyed the cows with a feeling not so different from jealousy. 'Chalo, abhi bahut kuch hai aage,' Lamaji got up and urged us on. Reluctantly we all got up and started walking, still looking around, trying to form as strong a memory of this place as possible.

## The valley of fools

If I ever have an automatic response on my phone it will be: 'Hi, you have reached CWH, we don't go to the Valley of Flowers or Everest base camp. For anything else, press 1'. When Frank Smythe crossed a pass after spending weeks in the barren landscape around Kamet mountain and entered the Bhayundar valley while it was in the middle of monsoon, he and his fellow climbers were simply overwhelmed with the greenery, the streams and mostly by the flowers. So much so that he called it the 'valley of flowers', a magical, mystical name unlike anything anyone else had come up with, and wrote paeans to it in his books. For the next few decades, his description of VoF became the basis on which almost every European traveller planned his/her trip to Garhwal Himalaya. The locals were first bemused, some even tried to explain that every valley in Himalaya is a valley of flowers in monsoon, in fact there are valleys nearby with even more varieties of flowers, but the power of the written word is too strong, and soon they settled down to taking everyone to Bhayundar valley. So many expeditions, trekkers and curious travellers went to the valley that they ironically destroyed the very flora they wanted to see. So much so that the valley has been closed for camping for a decade now. Disgruntled tourists started calling it the 'valley of fools' as they felt cheated when they didn't see as many flowers as they'd expected. But has that made people stop romanticizing it and instead explore countless other valleys full of flowers? A big 'No'. Everest base camp also suffers from the burden of fulfilling the egos of just too many people.

Next up was the 'medicinal meadow'. Apparently whenever the villagers have any pain, fever, or other ailment, they come here and walk barefoot in the knee-length grass. We were obviously not going to miss this opportunity and soon, with our shoes removed and tracks rolled up, we were walking, first gingerly, then with more ease in the swampy meadow. As the snow melts, the tall grass here retains a lot of moisture and that gets mixed with the oils that are secreted to form a potent medicinal potion. This was nature's laboratory and we could only wonder at all we might have never known or seen. Lamaji's expertise was herbs and he was like a child in a toy shop, picking up grass strands, showing us how the oil is secreted, and telling us about its pain-relieving, anti-analgesic properties.

After about twenty minutes of good fun we decided

to get out, put on our shoes and continue. This however proved to be easier said than done. The semi-sticky concoction was not going to dry off as easily as water, and without a towel handy, we city-bred explorers looked at each other helplessly. 'Get down on all fours and rub your legs against the grass,' Lamaji came to the rescue once again. And so ensued a hilarious ten minute 'funny home videos' episode with all of us in different stages of inverted dog posture, on our elbows, then rolling over to our sides, but barely managing to even get the grass to touch our legs, let alone rub them dry. And as it always happens, the Nagling women chose exactly this moment to make an appearance, and laughed uncontrollably again. Dilip, in particular, was the star attraction for his singular lack of coordination. We finally decided the oil was not going to harm us and we should let it be, our dignity was more important. The women were going ahead and we decided to accompany them and see what was in store for us in the fourth meadow – 'the meadow of snow and rocks'.

After about fifteen minutes, during which we barely looked down on the path as our attention was totally focused on the snow-covered Nagling mountain and its neighbours, the high and mighty, looming right in front, so close we had to crane our neck upwards to look at them, we reached the mouth of a huge glacier. How much can one take in a span of two hours? (Share our feelings by looking at the photograph on page xiv in the inserts.) It would have been unfair if it wasn't so stunning as to make our minds go numb. We were now walking on the snow, still in disbelief, trying to make sense of the scale of the glacier.

After the customary photo session, everyone wandered off in different directions, in their own thoughts, amidst a landscape no one imagined would have existed so close to the village we'd spent two days in. Soon we gravitated towards the middle of the huge snow patch we were walking on, ready to listen to the magical stories of this place.

\* \* \*

## *Reality check*

**Jahnvi Shah-Carey (with Nikhil)**
**Senior marketing manager**

*Not having any preconceptions of the bugyals was a good idea. The second one was unbelievable. It literally left us speechless. I remember most of us just silently sitting there, staring at the view, lost in our own worlds. It almost seemed like a picture straight out of a storybook, with a river flowing next to an endless bed of grass and birds flying and mountains around you, fresh air to breathe. Wow! What more could one ask for to rejuvenate! In fact, a couple of our fellow trekkers refused to move and insisted on staying back to soak in the sun for some more time, saying they would join us on our way back.*

*The next was another fascinating bugyal – the medicinal swamp. On our lama's insistence, we all reluctantly walked into it barefoot and left like hippos/pigs playing in a muddy swamp. After posing for our mandatory pictures it was time to clean our legs that were mucky up to the knees. Now came the fun part; obviously water wasn't around at that time and drinking water is like amrit on a Himalayan trek, never to be wasted on washing hands, legs, face, et al. So the lama showed us how we should rub our feet on the grass and clean ourselves. We definitely felt like the mules that roll all over on the grass once the luggage is taken off their backs.*

*The fourth bugyal was the least expected. When our day started, who would expect thick, dense forest, then beds of flowers and grass, a medicinal swamp and then snow to top it all. The glacier was so large and close and accessible. A few of us walked a little higher on the glacier and slid down a little. Clicked, posed, talked non-stop about how it was the highlight of the trek and went back to Nagling with fond memories of the day before starting our descent to Urthing.*

\* \* \*

'Can you see that waterfall there? No one has been able to figure out where the water goes. Elders claim there is a huge reservoir under the ground and it's connected straight to the Ganga.' Lamaji was pointing at a stream of water emerging from under the snow on the edge of a cliff and falling straight down in the ground underneath, also covered by snow. That was it, where that water goes, no one knows. Check out the photograph on page xiv in the inserts to see for yourself. Hmmm, interesting, but we clearly expected a more dramatic story and he could sense it. The hushed tone came back. 'Focus your eyes on the snow over there,' he pointed high on the mountains. And soon we could make out tiny figures moving. 'Koi hai udhar,' Kinjal shouted. 'Haan, Nagling ke log, to search for the keeda,' was the cryptic reply. We let him take a pause, build the tension, and resume. 'Woh kal se hain udhar.' No wonder the village had seemed much quieter since last evening. 'Do you know about the keeda?' A rhetoric question.

And this is what he told us: High on the mountains (at about 3500 to 4000m), there lives a keeda, a caterpillar-like being called yarsagumba. During winter it gets buried under the snow and dies, of course. But when the snow melts in early summer, a plant grows from inside its body and sprouts out from its mouth. This tiny plant is one of the most valued herbs in Chinese traditional medicine (as an aphrodisiac of course). This keeda is valued as high as three lakh rupees for a kilogram (latest price is supposedly 10 lakh rupees a kg). It's found primarily in the higher regions of Nepal and has been a major export (illegally?) to China. Now that those mountains have been over-exploited, the focus is on the neighbouring Kumaun and especially the Darma valley. For the last two years, the locals have been told about the extremely high price this keeda can fetch them and they have started to collect it. The mountains have been divided between the villages and everyone strictly follows the demarcation. But here's the catch. To get the keeda, the villagers have to climb up very high on the mountains and do so very early in summer, when the snow has just started melting. This means not only very tough and dangerous climbing, but surviving for a few nights at that altitude and cold. And they are paying the price for this with their lives. A casualty a month is par for the course. But the money the keeda brings in is beyond anyone's imagination. 'Nepali smugglers are misguiding the simple locals and enticing them to take this risk,' concluded Lamaji.

Imagine this situation. The locals in Darma valley, who till 1962 were involved in a thriving trade with Tibet and even had their own currency, were suddenly told that they will have to find different means to live. Overnight, the prosperous valley was left to fend for itself through its subsistence agriculture. But they took it in their stride and adjusted to this life, and to outsiders they were these typically content, happy-go-lucky people like one expects those who live with nature to be. And then after all these years, there comes an opportunity, almost a lottery, to get rich quick. One or two months of work and earn more money than you will need for the rest of your life. Some took it. And they do have more money than they can handle, or know what to do with (last year, the motorcycle showroom of a big brand in the nearest town of Dharchula recorded the highest sales in the entire state). That it comes with a cost will take some time to sink in, I guess.

We couldn't make out whether Lamaji was for or against the whole keeda economy, it was tough to take sides even for us, but we could see he found the whole thing 'risky'. 'Abhi tension shuru ho gaya hai. Some smugglers from Nepal already know about this and soon the mafia will come here, then it will be a battleground. So please don't tell anyone outside about this.' (By outside, he meant the world beyond Dharchula. We didn't, till now.) 'But humko dikhao yeh keeda please,' Jahnvi verbalized what we all wanted to say. He thought for a while, frowned, and said, 'Okay, Nagling mein.' We looked up at the tiny dots in the snow one last time, wondered how they had even got up there without any climbing equipment or training, and started to walk back. We wanted a magical story about this magical place, but were now the keepers of a deadly secret.

*Epilogue:* So why have I told this story?

Two things have happened since 2008. The government got involved in this whole business and took steps to regulate the trade. The locals are not happy about this and they feel the government is offering them a price much below the market value, but that's a different story. In 2010, Nat Geo published a major exposé on the keeda economy as their cover story. Although they focused primarily on Nepal, they did mention Kumaun and Darma valley as well. In addition, the keeda economy has now spread to nearby valleys and even in Garhwal pretty much everyone is aware of it.

Lamaji did show us the keeda while it was being cleaned up by the villagers. It looks very similar to a caterpillar and you can see it on the internet now; just google 'yarsagumba, the Himalayan viagra' ;-).

* * *

## *Raju, the Guide*
*Short mein bole toh, Darma valley supplies you with a lifetime of stories.*

### More reading
Some easily-available books and guides that I have read and gained from:

| Title | Category | Author | Remarks |
|---|---|---|---|
| *High Himalaya, Unknown Valleys* (2001) | Travel / exploration | Harish Kapadia | Along with the Kumaun peaks and passes, the three valleys are covered in as much detail as possible. |
| *Rediscovering Himalaya* (2004) | Travelogue | Chandan Ghosh | Covers Darma valley along with his other travels in the Indian Himalaya. |

### What to do in the three valleys
*Trekking* – Roads are being constructed but you will still have to walk most of the time to explore the valleys. There are multiple treks; here are a few known ones apart from the Darma valley trek:

Kailash Mansarovar – Yes, the great and the oldest trek passes through this region on its way to Tibet and Mansarovar. It's the traditional way to go there (most people now go by road via Nepal) and takes a total of twenty-one days back and forth. You can do it only through the government of India.

Jolingkong – An off-shoot of the Kailash trek is to Adi-Kailash (old Kailash) or more specifically to the high-altitude pastures and lake at Jolingkong. On the way you pass Kuthi, a village surpassing even Nagling in its history and stories.

*Rafting* – The Kali river, which runs along the border between Nepal and India is now being explored as the next big thing in white water rafting. From Dharchula you can start on an expedition along the Kali for plenty of chills and thrills.

**Point to be noted**
Darma valley is at the critical stage that all destinations go through: it's now more popular than ever and more and more people want to go there. But the valley can handle only a certain number of trekkers at a time and they have to be very sensitive about the locals' way of life, ensuring neither they nor their teams leave behind any bad habits or garbage. The government will hopefully try and come up with some regulations, but it's the self-regulation that is more important. Go in small groups and bring all your garbage back.

**Local service providers**
If you want to trek in this region, you can do so either through the government agency KMVN or get in touch with Laxman Kutiyal, a local organizer who – apart from organizing everything – will tell you all the stories

you need to know about these valleys. His number is 9968276771.

To stay: Dharchula is the last place with a government guesthouse (KMVN) and hot running water. From there on, it's best to stay in villages with locals.

Story 8

# Darjeeling Hills and the Story of a Brave Girl

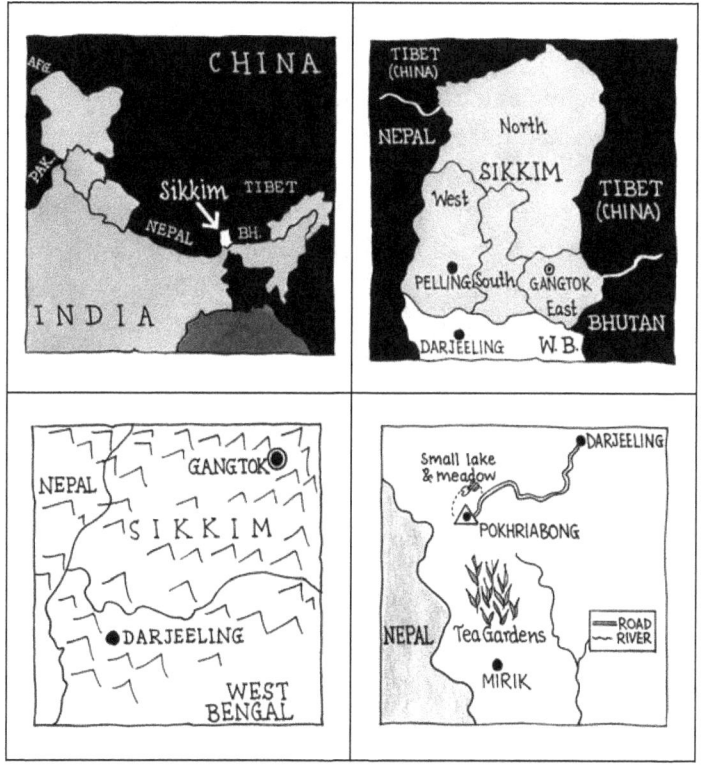

Hand-drawn maps for representation purpose only. Not to scale.

## *The setting*

Darjeeling and the surrounding hills, a land that is culturally vibrant, politically zealous and geographically profuse. It's where man clashes with jungle, native with incumbent and logic with rigidity, pretty much the story of planet Earth you would say, correctly, but played out with a bit more passion and with a bit more heartbreak in this jumble of hills, tea plantations, thick forests, tribal villages and proud people.

If you look at the map above and the location of Darjeeling hills vis-à-vis Sikkim, Bengal and Nepal, you can straightaway deduce that there has to be cultural intermingling and political intrigue in its past. Here is just one incident from recent history (in 1835 to be precise): Darjeeling was 'leased' to the British by the Sikkimese king in exchange for 'one double barrelled gun, one rifle, one 20 yards of red-broad cloth, 2 pairs of shawl – 1 superior quality and the other of inferior quality'. He was made an offer he couldn't refuse.

## *Setting the record straight*

But was Darjeeling always a part of Sikkim? Here is a simplified version of the complex history of this region in the words of

Smrithi Rumdali Rai of Pokhriabong village, Darjeeling hills (this is an account passed down the generations from her great-great-grandfather's time):

*Long ago from the* Mahabharata *days (there is ample reference of them in the epic) there was a bunch of people called the Kirats. These were people of Tibeto-Burmese origin. These people were also called the Shawn Mokwan. As a nomadic tribe they wandered around a bit and then slowly settled along the foothills of the Himalaya. To cut a long story short, there were two kingdoms to the east of present-day Nepal. The kingdoms of Khambuwan and Limbuwan.*

*As time went by, the Khambuwan and Limbuwan people had various kings and their territories grew and lessened under the various rules. At one point in time the borders of Limbuwan extended from the Dudh Koshi river in the west to the Teesta river in the east (Teesta is in present-day Sikkim), and Khambuwan from Dudh Koshi river in the east to the Bagmati river in the west (both Dudh Koshi and Bagmati rivers fall in Nepal now).*

*China, Sikkim, Bhutan and the East India Company have had their parts to play in the politics that happened in Limbuwan and Khambuwan. The Nepalese king Prithvi Narayan Saha wanted to unite all the kingdoms into one consolidated country and this triggered the decline of the Khambu and the Limbu kingdoms. When he finally succeeded, Khambuwan and a part of Limbuwan went to present-day Nepal, and the Sikkimese got the British to help them defeat the people of Limbuwan. The British used Limbuwan lands for tea etc. and paid a nominal sum to Sikkim for it.*

*Thus the lands that Darjeeling is originally a part of, the Limbuwan kingdom, ceased to exist after 4th December 1815 under the Treaty of Sugauli where the Nepal raja and the British divided the Kirat kingdom of Limbuwan. When the British left, Darjeeling fell within Indian borders and in the Bengal province, hence we now have to answer questions like how many generations ago did we migrate from Nepal to Bengal. We didn't; we belong here!!*

*(The name Darjeeling is said to have originated from two words in the local Kiriti dialect, 'dhulo' or big, and 'lung' or stone/rock which was*

> there below Mahakal Dara above Chowrasta. You can see it at a painting at Keventer's, an old, well-known restaurant in Darjeeling. Thus it is said Dhulo-Lung became Darjeeling.)

## *The stage*

In the heart of Darjeeling hills lies a tribal village called Pokhriabong. It has its share of forests, tea plantations, tribal rituals and such assorted qualities of a typical village and would have been an anonymous one, but for a brave native girl and her family. Smrithi Rumdali Rai grew up in this village, but unlike everyone else like her who had the means for a proper education and moved on to cities and jobs, she decided to stay back in the village and help out with what she felt is the biggest thing holding the locals back: lack of good education. She started Riverdale, an orphanage-cum-school for children from nearby villages who have lost their parent(s) or who have no means of getting an education.

With a brilliant self-designed curriculum which is a mixture of practical knowledge and its application in real life, using English as the medium of instruction along with a strong emphasis on understanding their identity and culture, the kids are prepared for higher education in their chosen field. In addition she has started a campaign to educate villagers against indiscriminate cutting of trees and linked it to the survival of the pangolin, an ant-eater found in the forest nearby and whose meat is a delicacy in south-east Asia. Save the pangolin, and you save the forests.

## The cast
Apart from Smrithi, her cousin Nazim, her extended family and friends, her twenty school kids, all the inhabitants of Pokhriabong and some from the nearby villages, and twelve of us, amateur runners and wannabe trekkers.

## The act: The day we ran for the ant-eaters
'How come there are penguins in Darjeeling?' Atul said – his idea of a joke – as we sat outside a coffee shop in Darjeeling. 'They're pangolins – an ant-eater.' 'Is there even a thing like that? Eating ants, wow.' This was just an exaggerated version of what most of us felt about ant-eaters. Which, to put it clearly, was not much. And to run 10 km in a remote village deep in the Darjeeling hills in their support, well, these guys must really love me, or more likely, were not sure what they'd signed up for. It was 2008, I had just started CWH, and most of the people who travelled with me were friends and acquaintances. Runners, in fact, as all of us were training for the Mumbai half-marathon with Rujuta.

Running was in the air and when I read on Smrithi's blog about how they had organized a run for the villagers as a means to get the community together and in turn give them some gyan about not killing pangolins, discreetly of course, I called her up to discuss this idea of mine. We were going to Darjeeling and Sikkim for a nine-day trip, including a four-day trek in Sikkim (next chapter) and were anyway planning to visit Smrithi and her school. So why not do a short run, ostensibly as a preparation for our trek but more as a means to show our support for her.

I always feel that people are invariably on the lookout for a genuine cause to support, where they are sure that their contribution is reaching whom it is meant for. While we were grappling with what or how to contribute – money, clothes, books, gas cylinder – Smrithi came up with an idea: 'How about donating pressure cookers to the tribal families. Burning wood is their only source of fuel, and since we are trying to get them not to cut the forest indiscriminately, which in turn will save the habitat of pangolins, the only way to reduce consumption of firewood is to reduce cooking time. And pressure cookers reduce cooking time by almost fifty per cent.' Wow. A lesson learnt for the rest of my life: whenever we take the higher ground and decide to 'help out' a group or a village or whatever, it's best to get the insider viewpoint on what is most practical and effective.

Cut forward to us sipping Darjeeling tea at the omnipresent CCD and discussing pangolins and the run the next day. 'It's a small and poor village so keep your expectations low. Smrithi has insisted we eat with her and the kids so our lunch will be there; local cuisine consisting of surprises, is what she said.' 'But I'm still not sure how this run will help their cause,' the ever-practical Janak said. 'See, it's like this. When outsiders, especially from Mumbai, come to a small village and support a cause, the message somehow is driven much better,' I repeated Smrithi's reply to the same question. 'And we are running because it's something that they have already organized once, so there are some locals who will participate, plus it's a good preparation for our trek and we are anyway missing our Sunday run this week.' I would have been convinced by these many reasons, I thought to myself.

So we strolled back towards Chaurasta and our hotel, passing the narrow lanes chock-a-block with pedestrians, vehicles and stalls selling mostly woollens and handicrafts, taking in the unique Darjeeling blend of the ultra hip youngsters and the traditionally dressed elders. Once in a while, on the left, through a narrow gap between shops and barbed wire, we could glimpse the sun setting behind a snow-clad Himalayan range and were reminded of what makes Darjeeling so special. The just-like-that sighting of a mighty peak like Kangchendzonga, unlike in any other 'hill-station' in India. That and the Chaurasta, a courtyard on top of the observatory hill, which is large, open and most importantly, vehicle free.

The next day began early, with us getting into the cars (which we had hired from Pokhriabong village) and driving till we were 10 km from Pokhriabong. As we got down from our vehicles and started some mild stretching, four shy boys from the village, who would be running along with us, joined us. Nazim, Smrithi's cousin, was the coordinator and he told us that there is lot of interest in the village about our run and that some local media might even be there. Hmmm, it was getting exciting.

And then, just like that, without a pistol-shot or any major flag-off, we started running. It was our group of twelve and the four boys – who, by the way, disappeared ahead very soon. With a straight face we spoke about not 'competing' with them but rather 'enjoying' our run through the beautiful forest. As if. But we were enjoying the run for sure; the forest was dense and changed complexion every few hundred metres, the road was devoid of any traffic, and the drivers that had dropped us would go past every few minutes, encouraging us and offering water. It was turning out to be a surprisingly pleasant experience.

The altitude though was a hindrance and quite a few of us resorted to walk-run-walk tactics. And even though Nazim had told us, we were still not prepared for what awaited us as we approached the village.

Every single person from the village, and many from nearby villages, had lined up in the streets leading up to Smrithi's school, and as soon as they saw us, there was loud cheering, laughing and shouts of encouragement. We were first bewildered, then amused and finally feeling like some major celebrities, started to wave back. Some even picked up their pace to impress the crowd. There were posters everywhere about our group from Mumbai who had come to run and support the 'Save the Pangolin' campaign. It got even better when some local reporters appeared and started clicking our pictures. If some of us behaved like Olympic tri-athletes, we should be forgiven.

* * *

## *Reality check*

**Rajiv Sethi (with Sarika)
Founder, Gemini group of companies**

*A motley group of people, with different levels of fitness, descended at the border of a sleepy village, an hour's drive from central Darjeeling. In spite of being equipped appropriately for the 'cause run', my size and girth gave no visible clue of my proposed action and intentions to the waiting volunteers from Smrithi's village school. They attended more anxiously to the fitter, runner-looking types from our group. The long-lens Japanese SLR hanging from my neck, resting lovingly on my Punjabi sign of healthiness and prosperity, must have led them to believe that I was the group's official photographer. And to top it, the absence of pepper in my salty hair may have supported their assumption that I was not one of the runners from Bombay.*

*And here I was, neurologically rewired to take on the challenge of doing the hill run – a complete 10 km stretch. A few stretches and a couple of swigs of water to wet my palate and I was set for the jaunt. With good tailwind behind and the pristine loveliness that only the mountains can offer, I set foot on the serpentine roads with reasonable ease. Ambling through at my leisurely pace, I was probably the last to reach the village and severely short of breath – and there was not a soul in sight. Damn!*

*But as I crossed the last bend, I saw a multitude of villagers and many a child cheering me on as if I were an Olympic runner – my first taste of adulation to my maiden running attempt. What a glorious day and the joy that came from every waving hand and warm smile. I bowed in reverence to the mountains and hugged GP at the school when I met him. He had a part in making me feel like a celebrity runner after all.*

\* \* \*

The final stretch was a steep descent, so most of us had to walk sideways, and then came the grounds of Smrithi's school, where we again pretended to run very fast, and finally the school with all its kids and Smrithi's family dressed in their best traditional dresses, to welcome us. Even as we embraced Smrithi and acknowledged the cheers of the kids, we didn't miss the four boys with medals around their necks, sitting bored because they had to wait endlessly for us to finish.

Eating the fruits given to us we surveyed the scene. In the school's courtyard there was a small table with some medals, kattas (a white silk cloth traditionally used to welcome people by draping it around their neck, very similar to a Buddhist greeting), and many boxes, which we recognized as the pressure cookers. The entire school (four classrooms, two dormitories) was covered with posters, hand-painted by the kids, providing information about the pangolin and its plight due to diminishing forest cover and hunting. This was one dedicated and creative bunch.

Soon many local women joined us in the courtyard

and Smrithi called upon twelve little girls, looking like dolls in their wonderful dresses. Then she read our names out one by one, we went to the table, one girl each put a medal and a katta around our neck and we gave one of the pressure cookers to one of the women. It was simple, efficient and quick. The concept and usage of pressure cookers had already been explained and demonstrated to the local women. And once we were all done, with big smiles conveying their thanks, they left. I don't know if we looked as hungry as we were, but lunch was announced immediately.

We went upstairs to Smrithi's family home and even as we picked up the different aromas while climbing the stairs, nothing could have prepared us for what lay in her living room. A huge table with not less than fifteen different dishes. Vegetables, curries, salads, rice dishes, breads – it seemed like the entire variety of the Darjeeling hill cuisine was on offer. The patient ones asked her to explain what each dish was while the realistic ones chose to eat first and ask later. For those interested, I've given a summary of the food there and Darjeeling cuisine in general at the end of the chapter (and a photograph is on page xv in the inserts).

With the good deed for the day done, and our stomachs full, we turned our attention to Pokhriabong. While running we had seen some very pretty sights around the village and now wanted to explore some of them. Nazim was more than happy to show us around, and soon we were out on a drive/walk in the hills.

Our first stop was a small tea garden and factory, then a picnic spot by a stream where they take the kids sometimes, then a temple on top of a hill (they are always at the top, aren't they?) and finally by the road just outside the village, where we got out and started walking behind Nazim. Within five minutes we were upon a most delightful scene, straight out of a trek in high Himalaya. Our path was a trail passing through a meadow with green rolling grass, no sign of any road or habitation and plenty of wild flowers around.

Nazim was being secretive and told us that he was taking us to a historic place. It used to be the royal lake or a bath or something like that. We reached the spot in less than ten minutes, and from behind the barbed wire fence we could make out a big depression in the ground filled with weeds. As expected there was a story behind this lake, of two birds – a male and female – who kept it spotless by picking up any leaf that fell in it, but then the male was killed by a shikari, the female died of grief and soon the lake dried and the villagers lost a source of drinking water. It's always the same theme: let nature be and it will support you, mess with it and you pay the price.

A quick visit back to the school, tea and some snacks, plenty of photos with the kids, promises of support for Smrithi and a warm goodbye later, we started back (photo with the kids on page xv in the inserts). We didn't speak much on the way, we didn't need to. It had been a nice day, in a fulfilling kind of way, very evident from the smiles on our faces. We still hadn't seen the pangolin, but we had made the tiniest of contributions towards its survival, we had met and interacted with a simple girl doing not so simple things, felt the kindness and warmth of the villagers, maybe even provided them with some laughs, and discovered the beauty of Darjeeling hills, the kind which tourists like us rarely get to see. All in all, a day well spent.

\* \* \*

## *Raju, the Guide*
*Short mein bole toh, Darjeeling is so much more enjoyable when you explore it with an eye and ear for its vibrant history.*

### More reading
Some easily-available books and guides that I have read and gained from:

| Title | Category | Author | Remarks |
|---|---|---|---|
| Lonely Planet *Northeast India* (2007) | Guidebook | Joe Bindloss | Covers Darjeeling, Sikkim and Arunachal in addition to the other NE states. |

### What to do in Darjeeling hills
*Trekking* – There are some easy and short treks around Darjeeling hills and also a relatively longer one over the Singalila ridge, along the border of Nepal and Sikkim.
*Chilling out* – It's a super place to chill out, especially in the off-season (January-March, and if you are brave, monsoon time) when the lanes are not crowded and the locals are more relaxed as well. You can choose to stay in the heart of Darjeeling with views of high mountains or in the middle of tea gardens. In any case, a cup of Darjeeling tea and a book is all you need.

## Point to be noted

Like many other popular hill stations, Darjeeling becomes very hectic in summer. If that's the only time you can go there, ensure that you patronize local establishments, whether it's guesthouses, or shops, or restaurants and not the 'seasonal' ones that come during the tourist season and drive the locals away.

## Local service providers

Smrithi can be reached at www.riverdaletimes.blogspot.in or more likely at 9733013845 and etriverdale@yahoo.co.in. You can visit and stay at her home, as a homestay, and meet the kids, and if you feel it's worth it, even support them by sponsoring their education or food, etc. She and Nazim can also advise you about some hidden travel gems in the Darjeeling region.

HELP tourism initiative is a good organization that works with local communities and engages them in tourist activities – www.helptourism.com. They also work extensively in the Northeast.

## *A guide to local food (Darjeeling hills) by Smrithi*

| Normal food | Weird food | Bizarre food |
|---|---|---|
| – We eat rice, dal, vegetables and meat like everyone else. Preference is rice not wheat.<br>– Some food we cook at celebrations:<br>a) Sel-roti: this is a must – fried doughnuts made with rice powder, sugar and cardamom.<br>b) Aloo-dum: all Gorkhas are crazy about aloo-dum.<br>c) Meat: the people here are mostly non-vegetarian and usually eat pork and chicken; we eat beef and mutton as well, but not too much. | – Stinging nettle soup (they say it is good for patients with a high BP).<br>– Fermented radish tops called 'grunduk' (tastes like the south Indian rasam).<br>– Kineama: soybean processed like cheese and as smelly!<br>– Bamboo shoots, both as pickle and curry.<br>– Pakoras made from pumpkin flower and also buckwheat flour.<br>– Pancakes made from buckwheat, maize and millet flour.<br>– 'Fiddle heads' of ferns (called 'ningro') cooked with cottage cheese.<br>– Banana flower pickle.<br>– 'Lapsi', a wild berry that grows on trees and is sour to taste. The lapsi pickle is a favourite with almost all Gorkhas.<br>– The palate of a Gorkha loves the fiery hot dallae chilli. | – Frog-hunting is a great sport. An average guy in a village can go at night and, armed with just a large burning torch and a long pointed wire 'spear', can spear about 250 frogs!<br>– Frog's eggs. (I find this really yuck). Jelly like lump boiled and fried. (Not toad eggs).<br>– Honeycomb with bee larvae in it!<br>– Pickled pig hooves minus the outer covering/shell (trotters).<br>– Fried wild bee larvae.<br>– 'Padhera' (don't know the English name of this insect). They make pickle out of it.<br>– River crabs and snails!<br>– Beef lungs filled with tsampa and spices !<br>We don't eat snakes! Thank god. |

Story 9

# Sikkim and the Art of Tourism

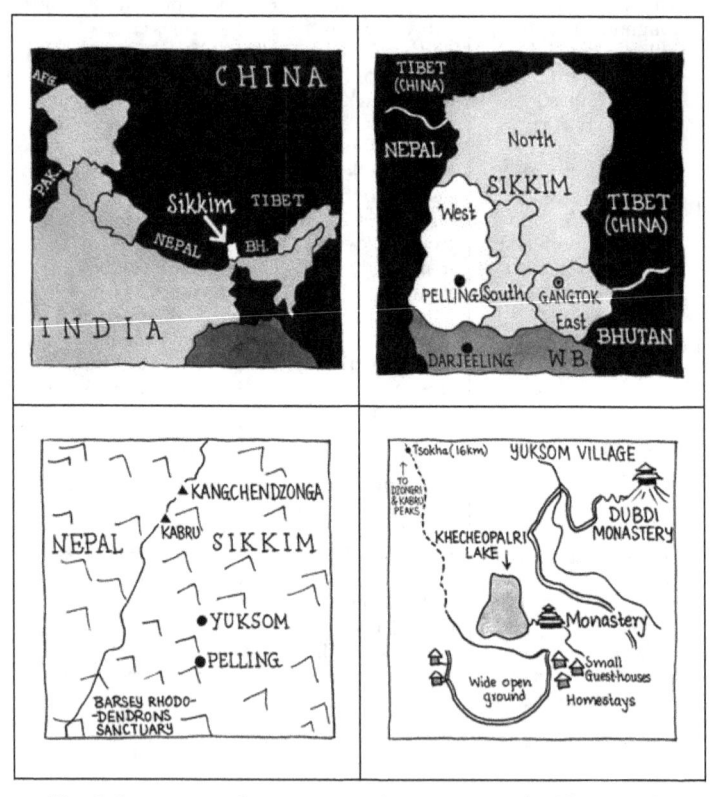

Hand-drawn maps for representation purpose only. Not to scale.

## *The setting*

Sikkim is conveniently divided into west, central, east and north Sikkim, its small size favouring a clear division and perhaps also the reason behind the efficient administration. As a state it has realized that its strength lies in preserving and showcasing what it has, rather than pretending to be Switzerland or some such thing like so many other Himalayan regions do. So you will find the best-run homestays, monasteries that strike a balance between being tourist attractions and places of learning, and village co-operatives being the primary players in organizing treks, etc.

West Sikkim is actually Sikkim in a nutshell: it has the high peaks and treks of the north, the monasteries and homestays of the central part, and the tribal villages of the east. From Darjeeling you drive to Jorethang, a sort of gateway to west and central Sikkim, and then through the thick forest and small villages to Pelling or Yuksom or Barsey, the main tourist hubs of the west. Pelling is more of a chill-out, family trip sort of place (and therefore the most crowded), Yuksom, a trekking start point and Barsey has a rhododendron sanctuary for nature lovers. There are many monasteries and model villages (a special initiative to clean and organize a village) in and around these three hubs, and along with some good places to stay (homestays and guesthouses), one can spend a lovely week here.

Not to forget the mountains. Ah, there are views of the mighty Kangchendzonga from almost everywhere and also the equally impressive peaks of Kabru, Kabru dome, Mt Narsingh, and many more.

## *The stage*

The ancient capital of Sikkim, Yuksom, is also one of the most sacred places in the state. And it is now pretty much exhibit A in the art of tourism in Sikkim. It is a sprawling village (not a town yet) in a wide, open valley which has long been on the tourist map for being the starting point of the quintessential Sikkimese trek, from Yuksom to Dzongri, a high altitude meadow, within touching distance of Mt Kangchendzonga and its sentinel peaks.

We reached this village late in the evening and were driven straight to the community hall where we were greeted by young boys and girls from the village, the coordinators for KCC, Kangchendzonga Conservation Committee, one of the many initiatives by the locals to promote responsible tourism. They gave us a brief about the village and the trek, explained how the homestay system worked, told us about ensuring our garbage goes in the right bin, and so on. We had never had such an experience anywhere else in the Himalaya and it strengthened our belief that change will happen only if the stakeholders, i.e. the natives, take things in their hands.

Note: All's not great about Sikkimese tourism though. Alcohol consumption is extremely high and almost everyone is drunk by sunset. Make sure you have a word with your trek staff about this beforehand. You don't want a knife fight between them while on the trek, high on the ridges (a story I will tell some other time).

## *The cast*

Kinzong, the coordinator from KCC, Sangey and Gurung,

our guides, the rest of the trek staff, homestay hosts including Nima, and our group of twelve.

## *The act: The trek cake and Nimo ke momo*
(Trips are not over with the completion of a trek, and this is the post-trek story of our Yuksom-Dzongri trek.)

'Nothing scares me as much as these damn leeches,' declared Arjun, the six-foot, broad-built Sardar, as soon as he crossed the hypothetical finish line of the trek and plonked himself down on a chair. Our hands held high for a celebratory high-five quickly came down as he removed his shoes and socks and rolled up his tracks to hunt for leeches. It was November, way past their time, but the continuous rainfall which had shortened our trek by a day had also woken some of them from their slumber. One or two were found happily sucking on the legs of a couple of our trekkers. To compound the fear, Ajit told us, in graphic detail, the story of his IIT friend who had gone to answer nature's call one night on a trek, and got a leech stuck inside his, err, backside. More than a tactical retreat from the previous night's camp at Tsokha, it was mortal fear that got most of the group scampering back to Yuksom.

As those of us who had reached earlier waited for the remaining trekkers, I had to quickly work out what to do with the extra day in hand. We had liked Yuksom as a village while on our way up to the Dzongri trek, but hadn't got a chance to explore it. Well, now we had two full days to do so. I got in touch with my contacts in KCC, the local committee that organizes homestays and treks in Yuksom. We would obviously prefer homestays instead of a 'hotel', and luckily this was possible, so Kinzong went about coordinating with the host families.

I joined the group as they were sipping their nth cup of tea, this time with pakoras. 'But will we all stay together in one home?' asked Kavita. 'No, each home will host two or three of us. There is a separate bedroom for guests, and it will be nice and clean. Plus we all will eat with our host families, and it'll be traditional food that they cook.' Some found this concept exciting, some were apprehensive, as is the norm. Everyone loves it later, so I wasn't too concerned.

Our guide Sangey came over and told us that the trekking team was preparing a cake and they would also do a small song-dance routine later. So we were to eat at our individual homestays and then assemble at the hotel for the cake and the dance. Four days of trekking gets you in a zone where a cake is the biggest delicacy one can imagine, and already some of us were dreaming about the feeling of chocolate melting in our mouths.

By this time everyone had arrived except Nita and Ajit. The news was that Nita was having a tough time walking, and Ajit, the loyal husband, was keeping her company. Nita had made the cardinal mistake of buying new shoes just before the trek and now they were giving her trouble. But it was the last day of the trek, and even the worst injuries and troubles can't stop people from finishing their walk to reach a place where they can take a hot bath. It comes down to bare necessities you see, the beauty of trekking.

And eventually she did turn up, hobbling, trailed by Ajit who had a torch in his hand, more to safeguard himself from leeches than to help her, we figured. We all gave her the customary welcome reserved for the last person to finish and after some group photos, we accompanied our respective host families – who had been waiting patiently with us for the last hour or so.

Rujuta, Vyjayanthi and I shared a homestay. It was a large house, as were most of the homes in Yuksom. Our previous homestay experience has been in Ladakh and Spiti, where we stayed in well-organized but basic homes in remote villages. Compared to those, this was more of a boutique hotel kind of experience than a homestay, not that we minded. Our room was large and had four beds, neat and clean, with a towel on each bed. The sight of a towel after a trek is quite an emotionally-charged moment. Instinctively each of us dropped our rucksack and grabbed the towel, eyed each other and the door and screamed, 'Me first'. I was obviously shunted down to the third position while Rujuta and Vyjayanthi negotiated who would go first. The bathroom was on the ground floor, a basic one, but who cared. We got a bucket of hot water each and relished it more than the most exclusive sauna.

So, we bathed, changed into a fresh set of clothes, and obviously were starving by now. The family – parents and their two daughters – must have hosted many a trekker because on cue dinner was announced. Rinzin, a vivacious young girl, was studying in a commerce college in Gangtok, as were most of the kids of her age group, and was home on vacation. She was wearing shorts, a tee-shirt, hair straight and shining, just a bit of make-up, chewing on gum, a favourite activity of all youngsters in Yuksom, and was overall a typical hep teenager of Sikkim. She led the way to her kitchen where we sat on floor cushions and were immediately accosted by the aromas. Both her parents were busy putting the finishing touches to the meal and soon started to serve us some of the local delicacies. 'Apart from the salt and oil in your food, everything else we grow in our garden outside,' the father proudly declared. 'Wow,' all three of us said in unison. The food did taste exceptionally fresh and flavourful. Rinzin took over from her mother in preparing some more dishes and we focused on eating with a 'bring it on' resolve.

* * *

## *Reality check*

**Ajit Naik (with Neeta and Aryaman)
Owner, Multi Organics Private Limited**

*I had my doubts about the homestay concept, because earlier experiences had not left me with a high opinion of the hygiene standards of the inhabitants of the Indian and Nepalese Himalaya. But my apprehensions were blown away the moment we reached the house. Built in the traditional Lepcha style, the house was well maintained, and the rooms were simply furnished but clean. Our hostess, a cheerful young girl, quickly prepared a dinner of momos, vegetable, dal, rice and chapatis for us. Relaxed and satisfied after the delicious meal, we were ready to socialize. Only, in this instance, socializing consisted of bombarding our hostess with a flurry of questions about her and her family, which she patiently answered, by the way.*

*I came to know later that Yuksom is one of the success stories of Sikkim tourism. The entire village was picture perfect with clear views of the surrounding forests and mountains. Unlike most Indian hill stations, there were no ugly concrete structures built by hotels and lodges to despoil the scenery. As we set out for our trek, I vowed that I would pray at the nearby Dubdi monastery upon my return, beseeching the gods to maintain status quo at this Eden.*

\* \* \*

By 7:30 p.m. we were done with dinner and headed to the meeting point for the post-trek celebrations (and the cake). Soon, others of our group joined us and almost everyone had a great experience to share about their homestays. All of us had had something different to eat and were passionately projecting our respective dinners as the best possible meal. 'The saag sabzi our hosts made was the best, period', 'Ours was the most unique dal you would ever taste', etc., etc. Atul, though, was the loudest, declaring: 'Our Nimo's momos were beyond comparison, and as proof, I am inviting all of you to our homestay to come and taste them.' 'Are you mad, you should first ask her, and by the way, her name is Neema and not Nimo,' Sangita interjected. 'But Nimo goes with momo and that way I can remember,' was Atul's logic. Anyway, we all accepted Atul's invitation, on Neema's behalf, for the next day. Right now, it was time for something else. The excitement levels were building up as the trek staff, notably the snappily-dressed Sangey and Gurung, were running around setting up a table, shouting instructions at each other.

Accompanied by cheers and clapping, the cake made an appearance. *'Happy Traking Cake'* was written in cream over the brown chocolate cake. 'We baked it backstage, hope you all like it,' Sangey pretended to be modest, very unlike him. We decided that the youngest in the group, Yash and Aryaman, who had jointly won the (coveted) best trekker award, should cut it for all of us. In the meanwhile, we requested the staff to start with their song and dance programme. They did the typical 'you sing, no no, you sing' routine and finally forced one young boy into a slow tempo Sikkimese song. While he was singing, we were distracted by loud grunts and 'you are useless, let me try' type of sounds from the two boys bent over the cake with a big knife in hand. We chose to ignore them for a while and instead listened as the trek staff broke into a group song. The next song was accompanied with a few dance steps, and obviously we were asked to join in. As we were just about getting into our groove, Yash came over with the knife in his hand and declared, 'It's a rock in the shape of a cake. We can't cut it, you try.'

'What nonsense,' Kavita shouted, snatched the knife from his hand and headed towards the cake with a menacing look. She had really been looking forward to the cake and had declared to anyone who listened that she would have an extra helping. After a minute or two, and after changing the knife in the hope that the first was blunt, she, and all of us, resigned ourselves to eating a rock-hard cake. The sheepish smiles from the trek staff didn't help as we scraped some cake onto our plates and had a bite or two, depending on how strong our respective sets of teeth were. Our condition however inspired the guys to rack up the tempo and a b-boying performance by Gurung provided the kick that the cake lacked. From there on, songs and dances, traditional and from Hindi movies, just blended seamlessly into each other and continued for a long time.

The next day was as chilled out a day as one can have on a Himalayan trip. In the morning we went for a stroll in the village; actually, more of a full-fledged heritage walk: Danny Denzongpa's mansion in the centre of the village, the sacred Khecheopalri Lake (wish-fulfilling, also the spot where Sikkim's first king was anointed) just outside the periphery of the village and the high street (we named it high street as it had all the interesting shops, a cyber café for the locals in the community hall, and the best homes with private gardens). This photo on page xvi in the inserts is from that walk. We then shamelessly assembled at Neema's home as if it had always been part of the itinerary. Of course she happily made momos for us and of course they were superb, even taking into account Atul's considerable ability to hype things.

The group was still up for walking and we headed to the Dubdhi monastery, just above Yuksom, and oldest in Sikkim (for some reason, everything in Yuksom comes with an adjective). The climb to the monastery was much fun as all of us, acclimatized to the higher altitude during the trek, showed off how easy it was to climb now. (Details on how exactly this happens in Rujuta's chapter.) The monastery was beautiful and colourful with thousands of prayer flags strung all over (photograph on page xvi in the inserts). The lamas were friendly and patiently answered all the silly questions we had and even did a prayer for us. The Sikkimese surely know how to make you feel special by being warm, by taking pride in their rich cultural heritage and showcasing that prominently, but mostly by just being themselves.

* * *

## *Raju, the Guide*
*Short mein bole toh, Sikkim has cracked the tourism code and Yuksom is a shining example.*

**More reading**
Some easily-available books and guides that I have read and gained from:

| Title | Category | Author | Remarks |
| --- | --- | --- | --- |
| *Legends of the Lepchas: Folk Tales from Sikkim* (2010) | Folk tales | Yishey Doma | Great folk tales involving gods, goddesses, animals and nature. A peek into the history and psyche of the locals. |

| *Khangchendzonga: Sacred Summit* (2007) | Culture / history | Pema Wangchuk and Mita Zulca | Kangchendzonga is more than a mountain, and this book is more than a book about this mountain. |

## What to do in west Sikkim

*Trekking* – The two main treks in Sikkim are in the west: the Yuksom-Dzongri and the Singalila ridge. Apart from the unavoidable situation of too many people going on these two treks (the ones in north Sikkim are severely restricted), everything about them is superb and they provide all the thrills and highs of a Himalayan trek.

*Chilling out* – Another great option to do is to not do anything in particular. Go with some time in hand and hop from one village to another (short distances help). As mentioned earlier, there is plenty to see and do in each village.

*Nature* – Barsey has the only sanctuary in the world dedicated to just one flower, the rhododendron. Well, to its six hundred or so varieties, but it is still just one flower. And it's a beautiful walk inside the sanctuary in March and April, when they are in bloom.

## Point to be noted

Pelling is falling for the lure of 'development' in the name of featureless, characterless 'hotels'. Though the lessons seem to have been learnt as far as other tourist hubs are concerned, it's sad to see Pelling, arguably one of the prettiest places in Sikkim, suffering this fate. You can help though by the simple measure of choosing where to stay and patronizing the right places when you go there.

**Local service providers**
Sikkim has the best and widest network of homestays and local organizations who can arrange your trek, transportation, etc.

For west Sikkim, you can work with KCC to organize your homestay and trek in Yuksom like we did.

Another very active organization is ECOSS (Ecotourism and Conservation Society of Sikkim, an umbrella organization with many smaller arms like KCC) that will help organize your visit and stay in the Barsey area as well as homestays in central Sikkim: www.sikkimhomestay.com.

Story 10

# Arunachal – a Preview

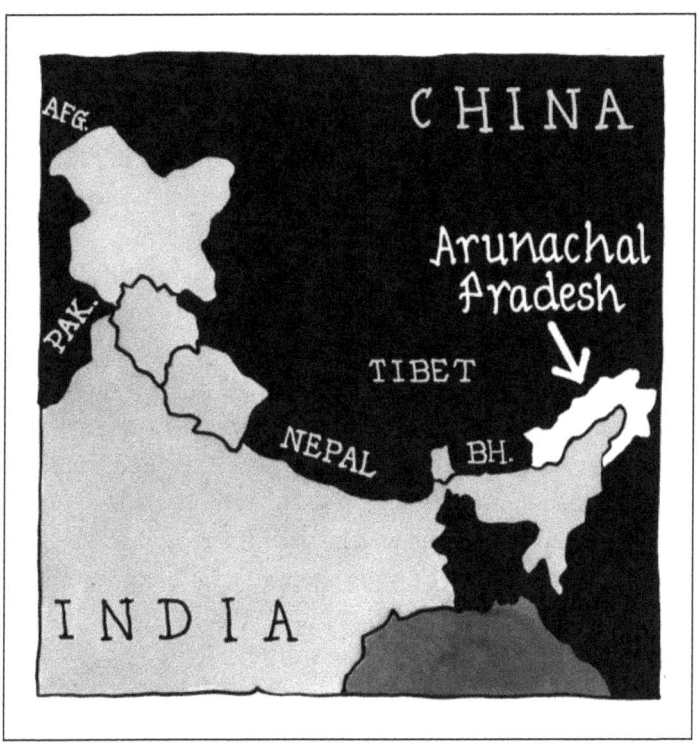

Hand-drawn maps for representation purposes only. Not to scale.

## *All-in-one*

What is an 'all-in-one' you might ask? It's the setting, the stage, the cast and the act, rolled into one section because, well as a writer I can experiment, yes, but also to give a glimpse of this region to the reader and to remind him/her that there is just so much more in the Indian Himalaya to explore, to find out about. You could blindly throw a dart at the map of the Indian Himalaya and go to the place where it lands, and it will be the best place you ever visited.

Coming to Arunachal, you can tell from any Himalayan map that it's the easternmost part of the Himalaya. The mountain chain makes a dramatic U-turn here at Namcha Barwa and ends, just like that. I travelled to Arunachal for the very first time in November of 2011 and here are my impressions (formed over a limited time with limited exposure and limited understanding):

1. It's a big state. So it's convenient to divide it into western, central and eastern Arunachal, geographically distinct and culturally too. It's the western part that has managed to fall under 'well-travelled' regions in the Indian Himalaya, with a road journey from Guwahati to Tawang and back as the crowd-puller. The infrastructure is relatively better, with a big emphasis on relatively, though the hotels and guesthouses are getting better and there are enough 'sights' to see on the way.

2. Make no mistake, it's an overwhelming journey, through the thick jungles before Bomdilla and over the snows of Sela Pass to Tawang, but it's doable. Get yourself a comfortable car and enough days in hand and you can

do so without much planning at all. Bomdilla onwards, it's primarily Buddhists and Monpas, the original inhabitants, and the monasteries and Monpa stone houses become the main attractions. Above Tawang, towards the Indo-China border, are some spectacular alpine lakes and all it takes is an easily obtainable permit and a car to get you there.

3. As an ode to the exploratory bent of the Hindi movie industry, a word you hear the most in western Arunachal is 'koyla'. The movie was shot extensively in this region, from the waterfalls (off the road) and the alpine lakes above Tawang, at a time when Arunachal was still an unknown land for most of us. The locals haven't forgotten it, and till date the main duty of the driver is to show you or tell you about all the places where Madhuri Dixit danced.

4. The Indo-China war in 1962 affected this region hugely and there are museums to commemorate the brave soldiers who died fighting a lost battle, and roads built to ensure it doesn't happen again.

5. It's the central and eastern parts that still retain the 'untouched' tag. The inhabitants are mostly the tribals, very friendly, and although in some danger of being exploited, holding on to their way of life. The mountains are smaller and gentler, but the forests are thicker and almost impenetrable. Adventure-seekers are having a field day in the jungles and rivers here, rafting and staying (read drinking and dancing) with the natives. Harish Kapadia is writing a book on Arunachal, and without doubt it will be essential to planning your travel there.

6. Coming back to the western region, I have travelled here and thus can speak about it more. I found the locals, err, amusing. Painting them with a very wide brush (and based solely on my seven days there), I am going to say that men are by default lazy while women are pretty and hardworking. What's the big deal, you ask. Perhaps I should rephrase it as 'men are slothful'. They start drinking after breakfast and try their best to drive tourists out from the dhabas their wives are working so hard to run. When asked the typical question about India or China, they take a sip of their cheap army-supplied rum, look at you and say 'India humein kuch deta nahi hai'. Anjali, one of our group members, had this response: 'In China, you can't even say this about them'.

    Arunachal is also a place where most road builders are women, earning their daily wages under the NREGA scheme. They break the stones and lay the tar; the only man around is the contractor.

7. Army. It's present everywhere and in huge numbers. Mini towns have been established by the army, with a thriving market, a community park, a school, etc. Most of the time on the road goes in waiting on the side as army convoys pass by. Well, in the first place there are roads because of the army, so one shouldn't complain. In case you were wondering where all the country's expenditure on 'defence' goes, don't look beyond Arunachal. But then you hear stories about Chinese preparation and the infrastructure they have and you wonder, is it enough?

8. Before crossing the Sela Pass, while you are still in the

greener side of the Himalaya, the best place to spend some time is Dirang and the Sangti valley. A wide, open valley with a river flowing through it, yellow fields on its banks, and yak breeding centres above in the meadows, it's a gem of a place. It is fast gaining popularity as one of the best birding destinations in the eastern Himalaya but there is so much more to it. Dirang is a town on the main road but has a charm about it that for some reason is missing in Tawang. The nearby old village of the Monpas, with its stone houses and intricate web of alleys, has to be seen while it lasts.

9. As you cross the Sela Pass, you leave the greater Himalayan chain and enter the trans-Himalaya, and the similarity with Tibet, Ladakh and Spiti becomes apparent, especially in Tawang and beyond. Tawang has gotten the lion's share of the largesse offered by the government and the army in particular, and although it can't compensate for the years of neglect, it has surely burdened the inhabitants with a problem of plenty. Everything is subsidized: electricity, solar panels, vegetables, kerosene, liquor, everything. More freebies, less expenditure. Tourism is now a bonus income at best, which comes with its share of troubles – service. Why would you want to work when you have enough just by virtue of being here, you get my point? So overall it falls a bit short on the warmth factor, compared to, let's say, it's spiritual sister, Leh.

10. So am I saying 'avoid Tawang'? Nope, just go with the right expectations and understanding of the people, their past, what they have gone through, etc. And don't

stay in a 'hotel' in Tawang, find a homestay or a smaller guesthouse and your experience is likely to be better. However, a couple of days are more than enough in Tawang; any extra days are better spent in Dirang.

Epilogue
# Trekking — the Way of the Wise
### By Rujuta Diwekar

*The rhododendron theorem*
*Benefits of trekking (OR how it helps you become a fat-burning machine)*
*What to eat on your Himalayan trip*
*The higher way*

'But the Himalayan terrain is tough, nerve-wracking and challenging.' No, it's kind, considerate and caring. The challenge really is you and your concepts about your fitness (or lack of it).

There's a reason why an ancient civilization like ours showed the wisdom to place the Himalayan pilgrimage at the Vanaprastha stage. When you are old or at most middle-aged, when your knees are not as strong, the strands of grey are visible, the wrinkles seem to be staying on your face … okay wait, don't get depressed. It's that beautiful stage in life where you realize that the body ages and changes, you don't. The phase in life where you are more mind over matter. At a stage in life where you would have dispensed all your duties, enjoyed all sensual pleasures and primarily gained two things (other than weight):
1. The luxury of time
2. The wisdom to undertake the journey within

These then form the only two prerequisites you must have to make a journey to the Himalaya – time on hand and the ability to get over yourself. (And this applies to everyone, regardless of age, gender or fitness levels.) The valleys, meadows, passes and mountains build the physical fitness; it's a by-product of the Himalayan journey, not a prerequisite. So don't ever let your physical fitness decide whether or not you are ready for a 'trek'. I am sure GP's writing has gripped you enough and you have learnt that trekking is just a glamorous name for walking.

And if you can walk from your bed to the bathroom you are physically fit to take the journey to the Himalaya, albeit the GP way. And no, he hasn't discovered or invented this way, it's the way of the wise, these paths have always existed, frequented by monks, shepherds, sadhus, sanyasins, yatris, yogis and the like. Now people like GP simply use these paths or their wisdom of gaining height progressively so that the cardio-respiratory system can adapt, of moving through beautiful pastures, meadows, valleys so that you can learn how vegetation adapts to changes in height, wind direction and sun exposure, and through villages where you can unlearn and relearn your concepts of gender equality, history, wealth and happiness. In short or short mein bole toh – paths which use interesting teaching models and are compassionate towards both a weak body and an opinionated mind.

## *The rhododendron theorem*
Hey! Sorry, my brief was only to write about how trekking or travel in the Himalaya helps you get fit so I am gonna just stick to that.

Now, to understand how the Himalaya builds your fitness naturally, I am going to have to introduce the *rhododendron theorem*. No, such a theorem doesn't exist, but using these kinds of terms gives rank 35-holders (or lower) like me a feeling of payback. So here goes, the theorem in two parts:

a) The height of the rhododendron tree is directly proportional to the partial pressure of oxygen or availability of oxygen.
b) The lighter the colour of the flower, the more concentrated is the haemoglobin (Hb) in your blood.

You know, as you ascend the Himalaya, the rhododendron tree undergoes changes in its size and the colour of its flower. It goes something like this:

1500-2200m: Tall tree and dark red flowers
2400-3200m: Shorter stem and pink flowers
3200-3600m: Barely a shrub and white flowers

Now let's say you are going from Mussoorie to Yamunotri, if you do that in just one day, and you can, because the road network is pretty good, you are likely to feel sick, tired, agitated and most unholy. The reason is you didn't apply the rhododendron theorem (RT). You have to have at least one night's halt at every variety of rhododendrons. You can't just go from red to white and beyond white where there is no vegetation; you can't skip the night halt at every stage. If you do that, your body doesn't get a chance to adapt, physiologically and mentally, to the changes in the environment.

We humans have a beautiful system in place that allows us to adapt and in turn get stronger as a response to the stimuli. The stimuli of high mountain ranges, low oxygen availability, cold, winds and unpredictable weather gives the body a chance to rebuild its lost bone density and musculature. It soothes the muscles of the heart, increases the Hb concentration in blood, optimizes the pituitary and the endocrine system, eases the wrinkling forehead, refreshes the mind and anti-ages in every sense of the word. But to do this you need to take the paths that have been in place since ages to optimize the body's response.

## BRO

The paths we take now are those built by the BRO. You know what BRO is, right? 'A cat has nine lives, but not the one which drives', 'It's always risky to drive with whisky' – the creators of other such profound philosophies for the road, these are the guys who keep our borders safe, the army's Border Road Organization. They ensure that there is a road that goes from Dehradun to the last village in India, Mana (beyond Badrinath), or from Chandigarh to the last village on the India-Tibet border, etc. These are the people who built this unbelievable connectivity, these engineering marvels, making it possible for convoys of military to reach the border in less than two days.

Now the irony is that time-strapped tourists travel to the Himalaya, use these routes for photo ops on Rohtang, for sight-seeing, or spiritual sight-seeing (Char Dham in eleven days) or take the flight to Ladakh (military airport again) from Delhi and make a big fuss about altitude sickness, fitness and the general nonsense that goes with it. The problem is that others back home believe it, believe that there is a lot of 'hardship, health issues and other hazards' when you go to the Himalaya. So they stick to the 'safe' route and do Char Dham, Ladakh, Rohtang Pass and still suffer the triple H. Triply funny, isn't it?

## *The benefits of trekking in the Himalaya*
Travelling to the Himalaya bestows many pathological, physiological and psychological blessings on us humans but we must have the stomach to absorb and assimilate them. And you all know that the way to get your stomach to function optimally is to sleep well. Now you see that's exactly where the problem arises and that's my main argument for following the RT. The Himalaya literally and figuratively takes your breath away and can leave you sleepless in the nights. This phenomenon is called 'periodic breathing'. What happens is that in the night when you sleep, your lungs actually slow down the rate at which they are breathing and every few seconds suspend your breath, as in won't breathe at all. This happens to allow you to accumulate enough carbon dioxide before going in for another round of oxygen. Technically this is in response to the low partial pressure of oxygen (lesser oxygen molecules available per volume of the same air as compared to sea level) to allow the body to match levels of $CO_2$ with that of $O_2$.

So this is your cardio-pulmonary system, your heart and your lungs, doing their bit to help your body cope with hypoxia (oxygen ki kami) and it does this by, and this really is my favourite part, building more efficient oxidative pathways; in simple words – burn more fat!

Here are just some of those adaptations your body goes through:
- Uses/explores newer areas in your lungs to accommodate for your breath – i.e. increase in lung volume.

- Builds more capillary network all over your body to make it easier for your cells to receive oxygen.
- Builds more mitochondria in your muscle tissue – again to help you receive more oxygen.
- Increases the concentration of haemoglobin in your blood – again to absorb more oxygen to beat that hypoxia.
- More red blood cells – won't bore you with a technical reason here, but essentially as more carriers of oxygen.

As a response to all of the above and many more physiological changes in the body, it becomes a much more efficient fat-burning machine. Come on, you do know that higher lung volume, more muscle, more mitochondria, more Hb means more fat-burning than ever before (muscles are the fat-burning machines of your body) and higher fitness levels than you can ever hope for at sea level. That's exactly why athletic federations the world over have disallowed all records above 1000m, because in the mountains you are physiologically aided or at an advantage to perform beyond your best. The federation sees this as an unfair advantage, an advantage that will be hard to replicate at lower altitudes or at sea level and will take the fairness out of competition. So now you know why the legendary Shankaracharya planned for this at the Vanaprastha stage, I mean it's with climbing age that the heart and lungs need some aid, na. And there is no better way to increase lifespan than to travel to the Himalaya. Our modern techniques of bypass, stents and angioplasty sound so nauseous and crippling when compared to this beautiful, natural and wonderful nature's gift!

> ## *Detraining*
> 
> Don't want to burst your fat-burning bubble, but just like the body adapts to cope with hypoxia, similarly when you come back home and take to slouching on your sofa, sinking in your car seat, etc., the body quickly adapts yet again to this routine and detrains itself (within a couple of weeks). Gone is that increased muscle tissue, mitochondria, higher concentration of Hb and what not. Your fat-burning comes down to what it used to be (poor and slow). But it's not all dark and grim – you can keep up with the physiological magic of the Himalaya by committing to regular workouts (at challenging intensities) once back home. This gives your body a damn good reason to stay lean, fit and young. The trick is to log your first workout within forty-eight hours of reaching home. Workout or lose out!

## *What to eat on your Himalayan trip*

First let's talk about what not to eat. We now know that to supply more oxygen to the brain (or else you start seeing things), muscle tissue, heart, lungs, in fact to every cell, our body will need to suspend its mundane duties like digestion. And it hopes that you show the wisdom of not eating processed, sodium-loaded food, which other than loading your stomach will also load the pretty valleys and hillside with ugly plastic wrappers. Just like garbage-filled hills take away from the natural beauty of the Himalaya, eating the contents inside that plastic takes away from your physiological adaptations.

At higher altitudes, as the air gets drier and as the resting heart rate increases, the body gets dehydrated quickly. One of the ways in which our body responds to altitude is by storing more sodium in its cells, allowing it to hold on to more fluids. Eating processed food that is loaded on sodium disturbs the natural balance that the body is trying to bring about and leads to bloating and swelling, specially of the extremities like the feet and fingers. Other than coming in the way of your adaptation response this can just take the edge out of your holiday because soon this leads to headaches, diarrhoea etc.

So when in the Himalaya, just follow these three basic guidelines:
1. Don't eat or drink anything that comes out of plastic be it juice or biscuits/chips/noodles.
2. Eat half the quantities (eat smaller meals more frequently) that you eat at sea level and drink twice the amount of water.
3. Eat local food – jeera aloo, dal chawal, rajma, momos, thukpa (so much better than instant noodles), kuttu ki roti, namkeen chai, local dry fruits like walnuts and apricot, dahi, siddhu, poori, etc.

Just these three will ensure that you are in a zone to let the body carry out its magic work and turn your body into a fat-burning machine. This way you will get less tired as you climb and also get thinner.

Some food items you can carry with you from home to optimize the body's fat-burning abilities:
- Ladoos
- Chakli
- Thepla
- Nuts
- Fruits and dry fruits
- Mathri

All homemade, of course.

Some people who come on GP's treks scold him for faking my involvement in planning meals on his trips. Which dietician in her right frame of mind would ask us to drink rhododendron juice (so sweet), eat potatoes (so fattening), rice (so much carbs) and rajma (so rich), they say? But come on, you know that not only is this misinformation about the nutrients in these foods, but also about the adaptation process the body goes through. Trekking itself doesn't burn fat, but following the RT and eating local is what puts the body in the right frame and gear to burn fat. Honestly, you don't need a dietician to eat right on a trek; then again, if you feel trekking is all about a free pass to instant noodles and endless chocolate, then what you need is a slap, oops, education.

---

### *Whisky is risky*

Alcohol and mountains, hmmm. CWH is such a party pooper that we have a 'no alcohol' policy. You may not be cool enough to understand that right away, but there is logic behind it, not some random whim. If altitude slows down digestion itself, how do you think the body is supposed to cope with alcohol? And forget everything that you know, alcohol won't keep you warm, it vasodilates, allowing more heat to dissipate through the skin and makes you feel cold, brazen and out of your mind. If you really want to feel warm, just drink some water, wear some woollen socks and go to sleep, the body will do the rest.

---

## *The higher way*
So I am not really saying that don't take the highway to the Himalaya, I am simply saying do it while taking the higher way. The higher way allows you a night's rest at

a progressively increasing altitude, allows your body a chance to adapt and your mind a chance to relax. In addition to the natural adaptation, following the RT also allows you the time and the luxury to eat fresh and local, and appreciate how cuisines differ over just a few kilometres, and how religion and culture influences food choices. Food does a very special thing to your mind, it puts you in a zone where you are ready to withdraw. Withdraw from the external world, the phone, BBM, cricket score, the BSE, the assignment submission etc. and to move inwards. Into the deep realms of your mind, to the reflection of the high peaks in the lake, the smile on sun-burned cheeks of a toddler, the colours of the puttu that women weave in the winters, the smell of the wooden windows on the stone floors, and inspire an unparalleled joy.

You notice that you have forgotten the days of the week, whether it's the mad Monday or the lazy Sunday, it won't matter to you, the mountain gods will still smile at you and you will smile just like that. You begin counting shades of green and give up this stupid need to number/count blessings. You feel like you are in love, for the very first time, and there is no lust, just an overflow of raw, pure, unmasked emotion. You cry at the sight of the morning rays over the Chaukhamba peak and you do nothing, nothing to wipe those tears off your now glowing, radiant face. Ah! The romance, the spirit of the Himalaya, it will hold you, guide you, lead you, follow you, like your own being.

Appendix 1

# Altitude Sickness

Outdoors is where all the action is, and no one wants to be left behind. Be it camping, rafting, snorkelling, rappelling, river-crossing, skiing, paragliding or trekking. Especially trekking. There are some excellent treks all over the country, and then there is THE Himalaya. The ultimate setting for an outdoor adventure.

With more and more urban Indians trying their hand (and luck) with trekking in the Himalaya, it was just a matter of time before 'altitude sickness' became the buzzword. An oft-repeated and oft-misunderstood one. So this is an attempt to put together what's known about it. (Notice the missing 'all'.)

| | |
|---|---|
| Concentration of oxygen | Remains the same regardless of altitude – i.e., 21%. So the amount of oxygen in the air is the same always. |
| Dispersion of oxygen molecules | Now, this is the important part. With height, the air pressure decreases and hence the oxygen molecules (and others) are more spread out. What this means is the higher we go, fewer oxygen molecules are inhaled per breath. At 3500m, for example, there are 40% less oxygen molecules per breath. |

| At what height | There is no agreement on this. Estimates range from 2500-3000m. Let's stick to 2500m then. |
|---|---|
| Symptoms | The most common and the first symptom is headache. The intensity varies. This is usually accompanied by nausea, breathlessness, dizziness, fatigue and an inability to sleep properly. Have any of these three, and you can count yourself in. But check this out: statistically 75% of us get mild sickness above 3100m. Generally (again there is nothing concrete here) these symptoms do not interfere with normal activity and subside within forty-eight hours. Symptoms do get worse at night (you are not breathing as hard). |
| What causes altitude sickness | Of course, the less amount of oxygen our body and brain is getting. But exactly how it manifests is not clearly understood. As per a report by Princeton University, 'It is considered to be a neurological problem caused by changes in the central nervous system.' (Whatever that means.) So obviously the causes are more generic rather than specific:<br>- Rate of ascent<br>- Individual susceptibility |
| Who gets it | Absolutely anyone. Regardless of age, sex, fitness levels and even those who didn't get it the last time around. So you cannot not be careful. |

| | |
|---|---|
| Prevention (Or rather – Minimization of risk) | Now, this is the important part. There are two approaches: <br> 1. Acclimatization. <br> 2. Preventive medicine (I am really not a big fan of this. How do you prevent something you don't understand the cause of?) |
| Acclimatization | The only way out (I think). Also translates into – gain height gradually. Give your body a chance to adjust and it usually does. I would add two more things however: <br> - Hydration (Add Electral and it works wonders). <br> - Food. DO NOT skip meals. <br> Build in a period of acclimatization if you're going anywhere above 2500m. (For example: Taking the Manali-Leh route exposes you to high altitude very quickly. The better way is the gradual ascent of the Srinagar- Leh route. Avoid flying into Leh as much as possible.) When trekking, your body gets a much better chance to acclimatize but still care needs to be taken. (And it's easy to plan as the height of most campsites will be known in advance.) |

| Preventive medicine | Diamox is the accepted medicine as of now. In short, it allows you to breathe faster so that you metabolize more oxygen. As I said, really not sure about this. Especially the practice of taking it a week in advance, etc. Too many contradictory reports and opinions. I guess its best use is to help you sleep in case of a mild altitude sickness. (Check for allergies to Sulpha though.) There are some excellent alternative medicines in homeopathy and some herbal ones too. See what works best for you. |
|---|---|
| Acute mountain sickness (AMS) | Whatever we discussed till now can also be described as very mild AMS. Anything more than mild AMS is life-threatening. But trekkers can chill because rarely will you go to such heights, so fast. It's generally the realm of mountaineers. Just know, however, in case the condition of the person is not improving, there is a realistic chance of fluids seeping out of the capillaries and clogging the lungs or brain (no clarity on how or why this happens). The only way out is – rapid descent. |

| My experience | From taking groups to high altitudes for the past five years, this is what I have noticed:<br>- Proper acclimatization (read gradual height gain), hydration and nutrition is the best prevention. Remember the 75% stat I mentioned above? With these basic precautions, you can bring it down to 20%.<br>- Awareness is the key. An aware person deals with the discomforts of altitude sickness in a much better way. (They don't panic, to start with.) |
|---|---|
| Sources | Internet of course. Princeton has done some good research on AMS. The Himalayan Club also has a decent booklet on altitude sickness. But mostly through experiences of fellow trekkers. |

Appendix 2

# Common Trekking Terms

Just because you see some trekkers (especially foreigners) dressed up in all the paraphernalia that the 'outdoor goods' companies have managed to sell them doesn't mean they are better or more informed than you. Trekking is about enjoying and internalizing the experience of walking through stunning valleys and meadows and no product has yet been invented to help with that. All you need is a comfortable pair of shoes, warm clothes and a poncho for the occasional drizzle (it rarely is more than a drizzle in the high Himalaya). However, what can make your trek more enjoyable is if you know a bit about the terrain and various features you will encounter on the way. So here is a non-technical guide to some commonly-used trekking terms:

A *valley* — Mountains on both sides, river passing through, makes a valley. The river is joined by small streams coming down from snows on these mountains. These streams have local names, for example 'gad' in Garhwal and 'chu' in Ladakh.

A *meadow* – A flattish piece of land in the mountains. Because it's flat, it will have grass which the sheep and goat graze on. And it will usually be at a height where it snows in winter (2500m and above). When the snow melts, it irrigates the pasture and lush grass and flowers erupt. Flowers in the high Himalaya are very small in size, but make up in numbers and colours. Different local name for meadows everywhere, for example, 'marg' in Kashmir, 'thach' in western Garhwal, 'bugyal' in most places in Uttarakhand.

A *pass* – A chain of mountains ^^^^^ has to be crossed if one needs to go to the other side. Logically, you will cross it at the lowest point in the chain, and that usually becomes the pass. Different local words for a pass everywhere, for example in Ladakh (and at any Tibetan border) it's called 'la', in Kinnaur 'khango'.

A *ridge* – Opposite of a valley. You are in the middle and on both sides the land drops down, usually to a stream.

A *glacier* – Snow that doesn't melt, keeps accumulating and over time becomes rock solid and few metres thick. It then moves down the slope of the mountain in slow motion. In Himachal, it's called a 'shigri'.

Appendix 3

# The Next Ten

There are dual reasons for listing these down – to give you guys more options in the Indian Himalaya (apart from the ten places in the ten stories) and also to give a sneak preview of what my next book will contain ☺.

Kashmir – Trek from Sonmarg to Pahalgam via the lakes
Ladakh – The Sham valley homestays
Himachal 1 – Lahaul wanderings (Miyar and Pangi valleys)
Himachal 2 – The Kinner Kailash trek
Garhwal – The Khatling glacier
Nanda Devi sanctuary, west side – Damarsain meadows, out of the map
Kumaun – Jolingkong and Kuthi village in Byans valley
Sikkim 1 – Neora valley, on the Sikkim-Bhutan border
Sikkim 2 – Thopta valley – the eastern valley of flowers
Arunachal – A passage through the heart of Arunachal

# Acknowledgements

Well this could run into several pages as without the people who travelled with me in each of the ten regions featured in the book, the stories wouldn't have materialized. So it's everyone who has travelled with me who has contributed directly or indirectly to this book. Thanks guys for laughing, crying, screaming, shouting, falling, basically being yourself. (And buying twenty-five copies each of the book. You did buy, right?)

Of course, our local coordinators in each of the regions mentioned in the book, for being a treasure trove of information and sharing some of that with me. And for giving us city pretenders a glimpse of the Himalayan way of life – with the nature, for the nature and by the nature.

A big thanks to Mr Harish Kapadia, for so graciously agreeing to read the manuscript, provide invaluable feedback and even write a foreword for the book.

Also to the usual suspects, Deepthi – my chilled out editor, Shreyas – my 'we can't have factual errors' illustrator and Rujuta, my partner in these travels and otherwise (good choice Ruj).

Must mention the staff at Khar Costa for making the perfect cold coffee every time (my brief was – like it's made at home), while I sat and wrote most of the book there.

After gazing at the Himalaya for twenty-one years from his village near the Shivalik foothills, Gaurav figured out what to do in the mountains once he started hiking in the Yosemite National Park while studying at the University of California, Berkeley. He completed his Masters in Engineering (Operations Research), worked for about four years in the big bad corporate world and after his leave count dipped to negative fifty, quit and started his venture, Connect with Himalaya, in 2008. It's as good an excuse he could find for travelling to new and unexplored places in the Indian Himalaya, meet and work with genuine local organizations and do his bit to spread the word.

www.connectwithhimalaya.com

www.ingramcontent.com/pod-product-compliance
Lightning Source LLC
LaVergne TN
LVHW020418070526
838199LV00055B/3653